Praise for *Workin...*

"If you ever want to know what is really ~~up, talk to a sex worker.~~ *Working It* is chock-full of harsh realities, hopeful activism, hot takes, sharp writing, electric intellects, dark humor—everything you could want, all from the culture heroes making their dollars at the intersection of all our country's worst problems. This is true outlaw writing, and the stories inside are of crucial importance for us all."
—Michelle Tea, author of over a dozen books, including
Rent Girl, *Valencia*, and *Against Memoir*

"A serious, eclectic collection that takes a critical eye to the tricky questions surrounding care and work within our society. The thinkers in the pages of *Working It* have a lot to teach us about both."
—Rax King, author of *Tacky* and cohost of the podcast *Low Culture Boil*

"Under neoliberal late capitalism—where wage growth fails to meet the ever-growing cost of living and the already-frayed social safety net is ever-receding—laborers in many sectors of the economy struggle to provide for themselves, their families, and their communities. Sex workers are among these laborers, and *Working It* offers what the editors rightly refer to as a 'kaleidoscope' of thought-provoking historical commentaries, academic examinations, personal narratives, and interviews. Interspersed with beautiful poems and creative images, the pieces in this collection, written by contributors representing a wide range of identities and experiences, offer readers an expansive view of sex work, while also highlighting sex workers' broader struggles, triumphs, and collective efforts. Variously confronting issues including but not limited to racism, classism, sexism, police brutality, consent, and respectability politics, *Working It* indicates the challenges—but also the hope and radical imagination—of workers striving to meet their own needs and support each other in a broader socio-cultural, political, and economic climate that is often hostile to their interests."
—Samantha Majic, author of *Sex Work Politics: From Protest to Service Provision*, coeditor of *Negotiating Sex Work: Unintended Consequences of Policy and Activism*, and coauthor of *Youth Who Trade Sex in the US: Agency, Intersectionality, and Vulnerability*

Working It

Sex Workers on the Work of Sex

Edited by Matilda Bickers

with peech breshears and Janis Luna

Foreword by Molly Smith

"Cyntoia Brown and My Black Body" first published in *Tits and Sass*, December 1, 2017
"What Would You Say to Other Girls Who Are Considering It?" first published in *Hobart*, January 2021
"El Cerrito" first published in *Twenty-One: A Story of Survival and Heartbreak Told in Essays and Poems*, Lulu, 2019

Working It: Sex Workers on the Work of Sex
Edited by Matilda Bickers, with peech breshears and Janis Luna
This edition © PM Press 2023

ISBN: 978-1-62963-991-8 (paperback)
ISBN: 978-1-62963-995-6 (ebook)
Library of Congress Control Number: 2022942729

Cover painting of stripper in court by Stephanie "Monty Monster Slayer" Montgomery
Cover design by John Yates / www.stealworks.com
Interior design by briandesign

10 9 8 7 6 5 4 3 2 1

PM Press
PO Box 23912
Oakland, CA 94623
www.pmpress.org

Printed in the USA.

Contents

Sex Workers against Work, by Adrie Rose

Illustrations

Acknowledgments

Collaborative projects are always hard: coordinating different people's work styles, schedules, and output is time consuming, and asking people to make art during a pandemic, when we are all stretched thin trying to survive, is the kind of demand I would think twice about now that I know what it takes. This book is the result of labor and love from so many people. I am so grateful to every contributor in here for taking time away from survival to create or edit these pieces into the forms you see here. Several people also did double duty writing and rereading pieces: peech breshcars, Melissa Ditmore, and Janis Luna, thank you so much. To all my friends and to Cathy De La Cruz and Shawna Lipton especially, thank you for the support!

Foreword

Molly Smith

It is an incredible honor to be asked to write a foreword to this anthology. The work here is generous, generative, and deeply dug in to the realities of sex work and sex worker organizing in the context of capitalism, colonialism, and white supremacy. These essays bristle with ideas, and they show clearly that the sex workers' rights movement is an intellectual powerhouse and is producing some of the most interesting thinking around, not only on commercial sex but also on gender, feminism, trauma, racial justice, work, and labor organizing as a whole.

Writing this in the summer of 2021, it is impossible not to think about the pandemic, which is still shaping our lives and still making precarious sex work more precarious. Sex workers were some of the first to feel it. Clients in the UK were nervous in early March 2020. When lockdown came, sex workers across the UK were stranded in crisis, without income from sex work and largely unable to access mainstream pandemic income support. SWARM, a sex-worker-led organization that I have been involved with, on and off, since about 2012, launched a mutual aid fund on March 13.

SWARM organizers thought hard about how best to manage the mutual aid fund. They needed to give enough to each recipient to make some kind of a difference, however brief, in the life of that person, but little enough that the money could be shared as widely as possible. They also wanted to ensure that accessing the fund was as simple as possible for sex workers. Ultimately, the fund gave out 1,225 grants of £200 to sex workers in the UK, totaling just over £250,000. Speaking to people accessing the fund, it was clear that many sex workers struggled to comprehend that, beyond the simple eligibility criteria set out, SWARM was not assessing their "deservingness": people were clearly used to having to recount traumatic experiences in order to be considered worthy of care or resources.

Equally, it was incredibly difficult to sit with the fact that there was so much need out there that SWARM simply couldn't reach. The money raised was ultimately barely a sticking plaster. As one SWARM organizer said, "On multiple occasions, people I was speaking to on the phone would burst into tears when we said we could make the payment straight away. Other things were hard too, like having to explain to people in crisis that we couldn't make multiple payments, or knowing that £200 was only a drop in the ocean for many. But being able to put money straight into sex workers' pockets for whatever they needed felt vital." One recipient said, "I went shopping [and] filled my cupboards. I am also due to have a baby in 4 weeks so I bought things I needed."[1]

Giving people money and trusting them to spend it on whatever they needed felt so crucial. In Scotland, where I live, the Scottish government gave about £16,000 to carceral antiprostitution charities to do a sort of version of what sex-worker-led groups were doing. (Umbrella Lane, based in Glasgow, ran a Scotland-specific mutual aid fund in addition to SWARM's UK-wide one.) One sex worker who attempted to access the Scottish government fund was told that the money would need to be paid directly to her landlord—outing her to him, and of course denying her any control over how the money would be spent, as if she was less competent than a child with pocket money. She ultimately did not access the fund. It seems few sex workers did. The barriers to access were evidently substantial.

Sex-worker-led mutual aid expanded the scope of what I thought was possible for UK sex worker organizations to do. SWARM reached people who they had never reached before. They put resources into sex workers' hands. One of the things that is so frustrating about the "sex work debate" is how easy it would be to actually reduce prostitution—by putting resources like money, housing, and safe immigration statuses into sex workers' hands. But of course the people who are obsessed with "abolishing" commercial sex through criminal law have limited interest in this, because it doesn't satisfy their libidinal desire to punish bad men (and, when you dig into it, often a libidinal desire to punish "bad women" too).

The essays, interviews, conversations, and art in this anthology speak to the work of the sex workers' rights movement as a collective liberation, with all the tensions and conflicts that that can entail. The work here speaks to a movement deeply intertwined with movements for prison abolition, disability justice, and anti-imperialism. As poet Diane di Prima wrote in "Revolutionary Letter #2":

> The value of an individual life a credo they taught us
> to instill fear, and inaction, 'you only live once'
> a fog in our eyes, we are
> endless as the sea, not separate, we die
> a million times a day, we are born
> a million times, each breath life and death:
> get up, put on your shoes, get
> started, someone will finish.

Note

1   SWARM Collective, "How We Ran a Mutual Aid Fund," Resources, SWARM's official website, accessed September 21, 2022, https://www.swarmcollective.org/briefing-documents-publications.

Introduction

Matilda Bickers with Melissa Ditmore

I was avoiding writing this Introduction with all my energy when my friend Josephine texted me that the prosecuting attorney for Washtenaw County (Ann Arbor, Michigan) had announced he would not be prosecuting the purchase or sale of sex between adults. Eliza Orlins, a public defender and candidate for district attorney in Manhattan, quickly retweeted and announced her intention to follow suit; while she did not win, the person who did has declared that he will not prosecute these charges. After twenty years of increasingly oppressive and harmful policies, are sex workers finally being listened to?

When I was seventeen, I started volunteering with Danzine, a harm reduction and advocacy group for sex workers based in Portland, Oregon. Danzine was unlike anything I had dreamed existed. Originally a zine started in 1995 by dancers to be read in the dressing room, sharing info about politics, sexually transmitted infections, and sex worker art and stories, Danzine was also a dynamic group of women who wanted to make their communities better and safer. They created a needle exchange service, planned art shows, called the phone tree of hookers who advertised in the back of local papers to keep an updated list of bad clients, and lobbied at city hall against the implementation of "pro-free zones" (areas of town where anyone suspected of selling sex could be stopped and condom possession was used as evidence against them) and other repressive ordinances. I volunteered with Danzine for its last year of existence, and so I started sex work with a solid grounding in local and federal laws around sex work, an understanding that sex work is labor, and a perspective of myself as a worker in a community of workers who faced specific forms of exploitation and abuse.

When Danzine went dormant, the absence was apparent immediately. Zines and blogs proliferated, but in terms of local publications, all that was left for the industry was a free magazine run by a club owner, funded by ads from other clubs and well-off local escorts. It was not a space to swap info about abusive or unfair management or bad clients. Two years after Danzine's closure, when a group of dancers at my club tried to unionize, we had no way of getting the word out to other dancers.

I started *Working It*, the zine, in 2015, at the same time I started the Portland-based outreach project Stroll, to fill the social, organizational, educational, and communal gap left by Danzine. The title comes from two songs that were popular when I first started dancing. From the beginning, I wanted it to be expansive and inclusive, with workers from around the country or around the world sharing their art and stories.

I debated whether to address trafficking here. Initially, I didn't intend to.

But this moral panic shapes the social and legal culture we live in, with very direct negative consequences for millions. The lived experience of the contributors to this book can only be understood in the context of the last twenty-five years of antitrafficking discourse and legislation.

The current conversation around trafficking in the United States is a direct offshoot of white supremacist fears that manifested in anti-immigrant legislation in the late nineteenth century. The first immigration laws at the federal level, beginning with the 1875 Page Act, excluding Asian women from entering the United States, and the 1882 Chinese Exclusion Act, were inextricably bound up with white fears about foreign workers and the sexuality of foreign women (Chinese, at that point). Subsequent immigration legislation doubled down on this, further tightening restrictions on which prospective migrants would be allowed into the country, based on ethnicity and sexual behavior.

The "white slavery" panic about white women and girls being kidnapped and sent overseas to be forced into prostitution was born of European anti-Semitism, but it proved to be easily exportable to the United States, where fears about interracial sex, and specifically white women having sex with Black men, added a new dimension: not only were there fears of foreign-born prostitutes corrupting the white citizenry, but any man of color was a potential threat to innocent, native-born white womanhood. How to address this was a subject of hot debate and many laws at the local, state, and federal level, but the most influential (and long-lasting) was the Mann Act of 1910, which prohibited the transportation or the facilitation of transportation of any woman or girl over state, territory, or District of Columbia borders for "the purpose of prostitution or debauchery, or for any other immoral purpose."

Despite being so broad (and thus open to manipulation), the Mann Act has never been repealed, although it has been amended to apply only to acts that are criminalized in the jurisdiction in which they occurred. As recently as a 2015 City Club of Portland meeting, I heard a deputy DA from Multnomah County cite the Mann Act. I was there to offer a contrasting view of sex trafficking from the audience, one that proved to be necessary, as misinformation was piled upon misinformation. Escorts blur their faces in ads not because of the legal and social repercussions of being outed, but because we're trafficked! A lipstick tattoo—like many people, including Tommy Lee of Mötley Crüe and my friend Danika's stepmother, I have one—is the new bar code of sex-trafficking victims. Amusingly (or not, depending on your mood), the deputy DA was referencing a woman's possession of condoms as evidence of trafficking. The woman hadn't crossed any borders, but the condoms were made in India: "Boom! Interstate commerce!"[1] This deputy DA was presenting to a City Club meeting, not a courtroom; I can't tell if he would have been as disingenuous in front of a judge, or if the point was more to intimidate sex workers unfamiliar with the law into simply pleading guilty.

So a bad law over a century old is still on the books and still being used to prosecute people. What are more recent developments?

Trading sex or sexual services for money, food, shelter, or other commodities never disappeared, sexual abuse never ended, and white supremacist fears about interracial sex never really went away, yet white slavery stopped being such a driving international moral panic for decades. The reasons for this gap are beyond the scope of this introduction (a reading list is included on p. 20 for those interested in learning more), but the reasons for its resurgence have a direct bearing on all our

lives. Globalization, increased ease of international travel, growing instability resulting from Western imperialism and ongoing exploitation of
the global South, which has forced millions of people of color to migrate
for better working conditions and wages—all of these have increased
long-held white Western fears about migration and, ultimately, the ability of Western governments to maintain their control and influence in
other countries. All of the factors that led to the Chinese Exclusion Act
and the Mann Act—the moral panics that drove fears of white slavery—
resurfaced with renewed urgency in the late 1990s, increased after the
September 11 attacks in the United States, and sped up after the recession
of 2007 to 2009 created or exacerbated economic instability for millions
around the world.

I want to underscore here the fact that women have greatly influenced every iteration of the national and international debate around
trafficking. From nineteenth-century reformers who vocally agitated for
new laws that would protect the vulnerable from abuse to the present
unholy union between conservatives and feminists that is leading and
fueling the current trafficking panic, women have had a large part in
shaping this conversation. Despite all the surface differences that would
appear to divide conservative Christians and avowed feminists, their
shared determination to abolish prostitution and other forms of sex work
have united them since the late 1990s, when they collaborated in shaping
the United Nations' 2000 Trafficking Protocol to inaccurately emphasize
sexual exploitation as *the* key form of labor exploitation. This unex-
pected union continued to shape trafficking discourse over the next two
decades, with the enthusiastic participation of the Bush administration.
The guise of saving women and children from trafficking—protecting
them from anything sex-related outside the context of marriage—offered
a convenient shield for the Bush administration's agenda of reversing
a decade of progress on sex education and sexual health domestically
and abroad. Funds for victims of trafficking in the United States were
restricted such that services for trafficked persons, even those who had
been forced into prostitution, were not allowed to be used to refer survi-
vors to reproductive health services. Abstinence-only education was
promoted across the US, while discussions around sex work increasingly
framed it as the result of coercion and exploitation. Unfortunately, the
conservative agenda affected US foreign aid as well, barring condoms and
reproductive health material and denying aid to countries that didn't

conform with US policies against prostitution, which the US government equated with trafficking. Countries that repeatedly failed to meet US metrics on "combating trafficking" could be slapped with economic sanctions that would only worsen conditions for its citizens.

The effects of US legislation on other countries are not limited to USAID or sanctions. With the passage of SESTA/FOSTA in 2018, sex workers around the world were affected by the abrupt closure of advertising and screening venues as websites from the Craigslist personals to the Erotic Review and countless local others shuttered.[2] The remaining sites tried to cover their asses with responses that ranged from understandable to absurd: my local ad board no longer allows even one pubic hair to stray into an ad photo, while Slixa bars ads for using, among other words, *treat,* as in "treat yourself." The fact that they're still making money off the sale of sexual services while enforcing a Victorian prudery makes this funny but no less maddening. Trying to navigate the pardonable paranoia of review boards while still creating an ad that men will respond to is a fine and entirely arbitrary line to walk, but for many workers in many areas, ad boards aren't even an option. Either the only local board is closed, or it's too expensive to advertise on, or it doesn't accept dark-skinned women, or some combination of all of the above. Street-based work has grown exponentially.

But *why* are adult sex workers affected by trafficking legislation?

While "trafficking" is defined in the United States as labor obtained through force, fraud, or coercion, in practice individual district attorneys, prosecutors, and police departments have considerable discretion with regard to where they direct their resources. Whatever the federal definition, the lived reality of individual sex workers across the United States (and in much of the world) is somewhat akin to Schrödinger's cat: we are treated as both a trafficking victim and our own trafficker, depending on the needs of the local police and the prosecuting district attorney. That disingenuous deputy DA who claimed condoms violate the Mann Act went on to cite other signs of trafficking, most of which were racialized and none of which bear an actual relationship to labor exploitation: fake nails, hair weaves, possession of "bling," possession of cash, and presence in one of the two main Portland strolls, where, historically, being stopped by police with a condom on you could get you arrested for prostitution and banned from the area for months at a time. Even if you lived there.

It sounds unbelievable, right? How did we get here?

Back in the early days of the Bush administration, estimates of the scale of trafficking—how many people's labor was exploited around the world—were exponentially lower than today because they were much more rooted in reality. The Bush administration found antitrafficking to be a convenient vehicle for its antisex agenda, true; it also found anti-trafficking to be a convenient corollary to the War on Terror. In fact, Bush himself made a speech before the UN in 2003, directly linking antitraf-ficking efforts to the War on Terror and creating a moral imperative to be against both.[3] Bush's 2003 speech is one of the first moments when we saw the numbers of people "at risk" of being trafficked jump (to 800,000 or 900,000); these numbers only continued to balloon over the next decade and a half. Try as they might, the Bush administration simply could not find enough trafficking victims to support the grandiose claims they were making to support the policies they were pushing—policies that, again, cut off funding for sexual and reproductive health education and services, as well as more basic forms of aid. Rather than dial back the febrile rhetoric, they threw more funding at their problem: more well-funded groups might turn up more victims, especially with such large financial incentives to do so.

The Department of Justice (DOJ) and the Department of Health and Human Services (HHS) offer information about the numbers of trafficked persons their grantees serve, as well as numbers of investigations and prosecutions of human trafficking: "From July 1, 2017, to June 30, 2018, DOJ grantees providing victim services reported 8,913 open trafficking client cases, including 4,739 new clients.... HHS supported 98 NGOs that served 1,612 victims of trafficking and qualified family members in 48 states and U.S. territories."[4] United States law recognizes different types of human trafficking, and so the DOJ and HHS track types of trafficking: "Grantees reported that 66 percent of clients served were victims of sex trafficking, 20 percent were victims of labor trafficking, five percent were identified as victims of both sex and labor trafficking, and the form of trafficking for nine percent was unknown."[5] Service providers emphasize that labor-trafficking cases and victims are not addressed or recognized. The organization that runs the National Human Trafficking Hotline explains this by saying that "labor trafficking cases in the U.S. are chron-ically underreported due to a lack of awareness about the issue and a lack of recognition of the significant vulnerability of workers in many U.S. labor sectors."[6]

Young people are trafficked for labor and for sex, and some choose to sell sex but are deemed trafficked. The people most at risk of sexual exploitation continue to be adolescents, and the people most likely to sexually abuse or exploit them continue to be those closest to them: family and friends. The child welfare system remains implicated in the abuse of children, sexual and otherwise, and the group of adolescents most at risk of trading sex are LGBT young adults who have run away from home. People have visceral emotional reactions to the idea of children selling sex, or to the idea of children having sexuality at all, and these reactions keep us from having the conversations needed to create a world where people under eighteen don't need to trade sex.

A note here on language: The many ways that language around trafficking obfuscates the realities of sexual exchange or exploitation are exemplified in the conversation around people who are under eighteen who trade sex. Eighteen is the legal age of adulthood and consent in the US; anyone under eighteen can't consent to sex (with some exceptions within a certain range in certain states) and are thus considered trafficked by definition, regardless of whether they're working alone or with other youth, are relying upon an older person for shelter and survival support, or are unquestionably being sexually exploited against their will.

Before we even get to the varied methods of research on minors who trade sex, we already see a blurring that reduces the specifics of each person's situation into the catch-all of "trafficking." But, as Samantha Majic and Carisa Showden show in their comprehensive analysis of existing research on domestic minor sex trafficking, the research gets hazy. Different researchers' definitions of *minor* or *youth* "are as varied as age 14–24, age 10–18, age 12–16, and so on."[7] Their findings on this are worth quoting at length:

> Findings about age are reflective of sampling practices *and* they intersect with social factors, especially family life and other facilitators into commercial sex. Notably, abolitionist researchers who collect their data from institutional records in law enforcement, child welfare, and social service agencies report that the youngest youth in their samples tend to be trafficked or exploited by family members, acquaintances, or caretakers. This is consistent with ethnographic research by critical trafficking scholars who also

report that parental facilitation accounts for some of the youngest ages of entry into sex trades. In contrast, a large body of research on homeless youth, including LGBT youth, consistently reports that the longer these youth are away from home and exposed to the streets, the more likely they are to resort to trading sex, a pattern that accounts for higher rates of participation in sex trades among older youth.[8]

Majic and Showden go on to say:

> The dominant narrative about young people's engagement in the sex trades implies that transactional sex is in itself exploitative (hence the TVPA's [Trafficking Victims Protection Act] automatic classification of these youth as victims of trafficking). Yet in prioritizing the dangers of *commercial* sexual exploitation, this narrative fails to account for the more prevalent source of sexual abuse of young people: families.[9]

The reality is, if you're being abused at home by the people meant to be taking care of you, running away makes sense. The total dearth of youth shelters and services means that many runaways who can't find adequate legal employment will decide that sex is something of value that they can offer in exchange for any number of things. Whether they offer it in a formal trade to adults willing to pay or continue to date people they otherwise wouldn't in exchange for shelter, it's uniformly designated as trafficking by US law, which simultaneously serves to inflate statistics and obscures the structures that create these problems. If you're an underage person hiding from abusive family members in Portland, for example, you won't be able to access any services until you've disclosed contact information for your family or guardian, who will then be contacted. Unsurprisingly, many young people bypass services here, preferring to stay on the streets or with anyone rather than return to their abusive families or guardians.

Given these unpalatable truths—and the reality that no conservatives want to spend the money to fund shelters and services for LGBT young adults—a new source of traffickers and trafficking victims had to be found. While the lack of funding for services for queer youth is a deliberate political choice in line with the religious values of the Bush administration, preexisting deeply held beliefs about women who sell sex or sexual services, old feminist canards about "false consciousness," and political expediency all allow many more people in the political mainstream to accept unquestioningly the idea that no woman or young adult would willingly choose to trade sex under any circumstances outside of coercion. If that's your starting point, it's not a huge stretch to then frame anyone trading sex as trafficked, and the people around them as their traffickers, in line with the anti-sex work agenda shared by particular feminists and religious conservatives.

Which brings us to the lived reality of sex workers in the United States and why it's such a huge deal that a prosecuting attorney and a district attorney have publicly announced that they will be prosecuting not only the parties buying or selling sex, but their roommates, boyfriends, parents, landlords, or anyone else around them. The United States federal minimum wage at the time of this writing is still $7.25 per hour, not enough to cover a two-bedroom apartment anywhere in the country. While some cities have raised the minimum wage—for example, in Portland it's $12 per hour—it's never raised to what's understood as a "housing wage," a rate high enough that at full-time it will cover rent for an average one-bedroom with more than two-thirds left over. Millions of people are forced to work multiple jobs, scrambling to make ends meet, only one financial emergency away from disaster.

So what's a body to do? When even full-time government jobs don't pay enough to cover rent and groceries, where do you turn to close the gap? If paying for college is an option, do you try to go to college to expand your options? That's not the route out of poverty it was for people born before 1980: college is leaving millions of people deeply in debt with minimal options to increase their wages, and in some states failure to pay your student loans on time will result in the revoking of the professional license you went to school to get. If paying for college isn't an option, what then? Do you work eighty hours a week? What if that's not possible? Or what if you simply don't want to? The violence of poverty is compounded by the violence of being overworked, under-rested, and constantly stressed.

Sex work—the sale of sex or sexualized services like lap dances and sexual performances in person, online, or over the phone—offers another option. It's not the get-rich-quick easy money that people believe: even the workers with the highest hourly rates live through stressful dry seasons when there simply aren't clients knocking, while strip clubs illegally take large cuts of dancers' money without paying a wage—a slow night can end with you leaving in debt to the club. Over the course of a series of slow nights or even a bad month, that debt can snowball to the point where it may not be worth returning to the club. It's often hard and emotionally taxing work—and because it is *work*, it has the potential to be exploitative. A common refrain in the sex workers' rights movement is "sex work is not sex trafficking," which, while understandable, misses the point! But it does offer a flexible schedule and a range of prices for services that vary with the local sex economy but are *always* above minimum wage, and over time, even with dry spells, it can offer an income equivalent to, or higher than, a housing wage. It just makes sense. If you're someone who doesn't mind being physically intimate with strangers (and so many people do this for free!), why *not* get paid for it? To paraphrase the immortal words of Salt-N-Pepa, why *not* "use what you got to get whatever you don't got"?

There are so many ways in which capitalism limits our lives, but sex work offers some space to make capitalism pay off.

I do not want to be misunderstood here as espousing some kind of girlboss "sex work is empowering" narrative. The sex industry is a microcosm of the society around us: it replicates—and in some cases exacerbates—existing power structures. Many porn companies, ad boards, and strip clubs enforce white supremacist and heterosexist standards by barring dark-skinned women and trans women or limiting their access to good shifts. Customers and clients come to sex work spaces with these biases intact and don't shy away from displaying their prejudices even to our faces. Other workers can exploit racism and colorism to their own benefit. If a sex worker gets arrested, she is more likely to face criminal charges if she's a woman of color. Working in the sex industry leaves one vulnerable to violence from customers and police and the structural violence of losing housing, child custody, scholarships, or day jobs. It's not some walk in the park.

With all this said, for many of us it's *still* a better option than anything else. For some disabled workers, it's the only option that allows them to generate a living income without risking their benefits. For many trans women, it's one of very few employment options.

Capitalism limits our lives in so many ways, centering whiteness and patriarchy and pushing everyone else to the margins, without access to secure shelter, food, or leisure time. Trading sex can be a way for people who aren't meant to survive or prosper to do exactly that. We have to be creative, operating outside the protections of the law and the socially sanctioned, but this position both outside and deeply embedded within society offers a vantage point to see other possibilities and create new relationships.

That's what I'm interested in, and those are the stories I want to hear and read. I'm constantly hungry for the experiences of people who were faced with shitty options and a world that wasn't interested in their success or even survival but who did survive anyway. People who use what we have to get what we don't. While anti-sex work feminists see trading sex as the ultimate concession to patriarchy, I see it as a refusal. A refusal to accept the terms we've been given, to accept the violence of poverty, exhaustion, and overwork, to accept the limited options and future we're meant to be content with. In that refusal is an affirmation of our right to exist, of our right to survive, and the possibility of a reality without white supremacy or capitalism. Again, this is not because sex work is inherently radical and empowering—it's a job like any other job, with the potential to be exploitative or fulfilling based on the day and interaction and context—but because alternative economies can illustrate alternative ways of interacting. Sex workers are pioneers of mutual aid, for example: without social security, family, or other safety nets, we often have only each other. Sex workers in eighteenth-century England and early-twentieth-century Kenya provide some examples of the ways that sex workers pooled resources and strengthened intracommunal ties when familial and social help was otherwise unavailable.[10]

Working It is not a representative collection of sex worker experiences; as Juno Mac and Molly Smith point out in *Revolting Prostitutes*, such a collection would be impossible. Rather, it's a kaleidoscope of work that spans several genres and mediums, functioning as an archive of some of the art, experiences, and many ways of thinking, feeling, and being in our community.

From the first historians of sex workers and an examination of the liminal space that sex workers occupy in fiction as well as reality to a conversation with a First Nations former sex worker about the Canadian child welfare system and beyond, everyone responded to my request for their participation differently. I want to give you something of the feel of the warm, anarchic camaraderie of the work space on a good night, so as well as illustrations, you'll find short interviews spread between the chapters, some by contributors and some by other sex workers who were unable to contribute because of time constraints and the chaos of trying to survive in a pandemic. Each interview is paired with a picture of the subject's choice; some chose pictures of themselves, while others chose art they made. Some contributors responded to the text chapters, so throughout the book there are occasional notes that offer a chance to further interact with both the text proper and the sex workers responding to it. I don't agree with every opinion expressed in this book, but it's vitally important to me that this book function as an archive for a community, including voices that are not traditionally granted space in publishing or the art world.

Forced to the margins of society by the stigmatized and often criminalized nature of our work, sex workers appear to occupy—and frequently cross—both literal and metaphorical borderlands. These myths of sex worker as boundary crosser crop up again and again, inextricably intertwined with fears about migrants, women outside the household, and sex.

The shadows of the borderland can conceal more than unknown threats: they also offer protection for other, experimental ways of living, as Leila Raven discusses in "Sex Work, Care Work, and Prefigurative Politics." From outside the bounds of straight existence, including outside the strictures of the heteronormative nuclear family, Leila is able to practice new ways of raising and relating to her daughter, ways that support her daughter's autonomy and personhood and that are in line with Leila's radical values. Leila quotes Saidiya Hartman from *Wayward Lives, Beautiful Experiments*: "The mutuality and creativity necessary to sustain living in the context of intermittent wages, controlled depletion, economic exclusion, coercion, and antiblack violence often bordered on the extralegal and criminal," adding, "Black queer and trans people who have traded sex for resources create new norms out of necessity."

From life outside the space created by sex work, with "The Monotony of Sex Work," Sarah returns us to the reality of sex work as *work*: the emotional labor of managing boredom and disgust and performing attraction while also performing physical labor. The tension of life at the margins and with unstable income, and the things we do to grab that unstable income, are palpable, rendered more visceral by anxieties that clients do not even bother to try to manage, anxieties around being attracted to trans women and paying for sex with trans women and what these say about their masculinity and desires. As Sarah points out: tedious.

Former Soldiers of Pole organizer Domino Rey talks about the struggles within sex worker organizing, highlighting what will become recurring themes of worker competition, scarcity, and white supremacy. These issues continue to interfere with the potential for creating a sense of solidarity between sex workers, acting as ongoing barriers even to what would appear to be obvious points of unity.

When it comes to tedium, it's all about what we can bear. The monotony of waiting in a dressing room reading or watching trash TV is very different from the monotony of a legit job, where the boss wants to make sure they're getting their hourly money's worth out of you at all times and the bathroom is the only place to reclaim your time. In "Waiting to Be Rescued from My Office Job," Emily Dall'Ora Warfield compares the grinding boredom of her desk job to the anxiety over the instability of sex work. Boredom and lack of autonomy—which she says began as "tolerable," or at least "preferable to the poverty and ceaseless anxiety of unemployment"—take a different kind of toll than sex work, but they do take a toll. Emily observes that "Needing to work to survive is a kind of coercion anathema to consent. It's not a problem we can criminalize our way out of." As long as people need money to live, they'll be forced to do things they don't want to do to survive, and the current climate of extractive capitalism requires extracting the most work out of people for the lowest return, for the profit of a handful. This is not a setup that results in a healthy population.

Melissa Ditmore elucidates the toll that extractive capitalism—in this case, human workers are the resource that cheap labor is being extracted from—takes on all workers in "The High Cost of Cheap Labor":

> Fast food and other low-wage work shows how the demand for cheap labor has skewed the American labor market so that workers may turn to sex work or federal benefits to supplement their meager wages that have stagnated for nearly fifty years while executive compensation has risen disproportionately.

With so many workers forced to work multiple jobs simply to augment the minimum wage paid in each position (or less, in the case of independent contractors), it's no wonder that sex work looks appealing. The COVID pandemic, however, has resulted in a flooded market, as desperate workers turn to OnlyFans, camming, and even, at a last resort, the newly extra-dangerous in-person sex work. Now the stakes are higher than ever: with no fallback job to supplement a bad sex work shift, in-person workers are forced to take greater risks: being robbed, being assaulted, catching COVID, or, in worst-case scenarios, all three. Ditmore connects the domino effect that low-wage labor in one sector has on other sectors, all enabled by the gutted workers' rights of the last few decades.

In "Cyntoia Brown and My Black Body," Naomi thinks about the parallels between her own experiences trading sex as a young person and those of Cyntoia Brown and Chrystul Kizer. All three dealt with abuse and traded sex at a young age, forced to by the limitations around what a minor can do to survive. Naomi dwells on the "insane luck" that allowed her to make it through her life without being arrested and the moments when, despite fearing for her life, she didn't call the police, knowing, as Cyntoia and Chrystul knew, that the police would be on the side of the men abusing her and that her whole future would disappear into the US prison system. Examining the poverty that makes sex work look appealing to so many, Naomi points out that even these narratives have a sense of choice and agency that Cyntoia, Chrystul, and Naomi all lacked as sexually exploited youth.

Stephanie's poem "What Would You Say to Other Girls Who Are Considering It?" looks at the power imbalances between different sectors of the sex industry and at who can make money doing what. Stephanie's reference to a celebrity discussing her OnlyFans recalls Melissa Ditmore's dropping of this bitter fact:

> One person in the top 20 percent of earners on the OnlyFans platform explained that even though she is a high earner, her income from this platform would not cover most people's rent. She has not made $500 in a month, and she explained that the top 2 percent earn between $2,000 and $4,000 per month, while the top 0.01 percent receive tens of thousands of dollars per month.

The rest of us, those not in the top 2 percent even, are forced into closer proximity with our clients, negotiating boundaries in a way the rich rarely have to do: they simply don't feel the same economic pressures. The rest of us remain an interchangeable mass, disposable, as evidenced by the police phrase "NHI"—no humans involved—used for crimes involving houseless people, sex workers, drug users, and people at the center of this very vulnerable Venn diagram.

All work takes a toll, but particularly intensive service work demanding massive amounts of emotional labor, especially knowing that your murder, if it occurs, will be dismissed as "NHI." With "What Did Sex Work Take from You—and How Can You Get It Back?" peech breshears explores freedom and the connections between people and within our own minds that trap us. Financial freedom, the freedom from constantly worrying about money, offers an unimaginable lightness of being to those of us unused to it. Sex work by its nature is an unstable income, dependent on the ebb and flow of client desire. We're constantly having to enforce our boundaries against the push of that client desire. When the money runs short, we have to blur our boundaries to maintain a chance at that goal of financial freedom (or at least survival), and this blurring of boundaries—when it isn't outright bending—takes a toll. What does it do to a body, to a person, to constantly be enforcing boundaries or, worse, weighing the financial pros and psychic cons of breaking them? How do we manage that stress so it doesn't trap us in a different way, leaving us to reenact our worst relationship patterns over and over?

Looking back at their early adolescence in "first, last, my only," xaxum omer describes moving from place to place with their mom and helping her with her new job as a phone sex operator. Seen from their young eyes, phone sex is just one more weird thing adult men do, and helping your mom is a necessary part of surviving together as a family in a world hostile to low-income single mothers and people of color; later, however, they find that this blurring of boundaries comes with a cost. This piece is the only work in this anthology to have a trigger warning: an anthology of sex work necessarily deals in "adult" material, but "first, last, my only" relates episodes of domestic violence and sexual assault that xaxum survived.

In "Respectability Politics by Any Other Name," Janis Luna dissects the many ways we repackage sex work to make it more palatable—to clients, our families and friends, and ourselves. From Constance Wu claiming sex workers are "just like athletes" to the common refrain that "sex workers are therapists," Luna highlights the ways these repackagings ultimately work to restigmatize sex work, by treating the "sex" part as something to be excused or otherwise explained away, when it's actually the focal point of the work. Sex work is not therapy: therapy is therapy. Both can be affirming, but clients come to us to see their best and most desirable—or worst, and most worthy of punishment—selves reflected back at them; if we offered the constructive feedback a therapist is paid to offer, many clients would leave and never come back.

The sex Nick has in "El Cerrito" is certainly work, and hard work at that. Nick looks back at one of their early clients, vividly evoking the loneliness of the moment, the isolation of being alone with a client and wondering how to make it through the block of time until you can leave. If you can do it without revealing revulsion. If he'll hurt you. Even if you'll survive. If the exchange is worth it. Nick finds the exchange isn't always worth it.

Cisqo Thyme takes us to the bitterly frivolous heart of sex worker humor with her listicle "6 gifts you can ask your sugar daddy for that won't destroy his sense of your 'quirk' as unthreatening sexual garnish and that won't make you feel like you have turned into a cartoon glyph with tits animated by the dispossessed spirit of capitalist alienation." Each item is accompanied by commentary that vividly drives home the absurdity of not simply tipping your service worker money they can spend on what they really need, rather than trying to force further intimacy through gift giving.

Enthusiastic consent is something we hear a lot about, but where does that leave sex workers, who are only there for the money? Phoenix Calida, for one, doesn't like this metric, and she elaborates on her initial title, "I Don't Consent to Enthusiastic Consent," with the many ways "enthusiastic consent" is limiting and does us all a disservice. Like Charlotte Shane in "'Getting Away' with Hating It: Consent in the Context of Sex Work" on *Tits and Sass*, or Katherine Angel in *Tomorrow Sex Will Be Good Again*, Phoenix complicates the conversation around consent and enthusiastic consent, pointing out that by the standards of "enthusiastic consent," all full-service sex workers are being raped. (And what does that mean for when we actually *are* assaulted? Does that then not count?) She asks:

> Where does this leave me? Where does this leave my trauma? Where does this leave the sex work community? Under enthusiastic consent, there is no nuance. I am told there is no useful distinction between discussing an instance of nonenthusiastic

consent and flat-out rape because—in theory—these experiences are the same. I didn't give enthusiastic consent when I was paid. I didn't give any consent when I was raped. But as long as all consent must be enthusiastic, neither of these scenarios are truly deemed consensual.

Phoenix roundly rejects this framework.

Alyssa Pariah highlights the limitations of consent in a different way in her piece, "When My Mom Found My Craigslist Ad." For Alyssa, growing up trans in an unsupportive environment, sex work to pay for transitioning was a matter of survival:

> All this is the stuff of preparation for prostitution at a young age. Sex, gender, money: these three are tangled in knots that I haven't even tried to unravel yet. I learned about fetishism for shemales when I got the Internet, and sold my cock and ass for money so I could pay for feminization. But this is a serious trauma that I didn't consider would cause a lasting stress disorder. My mother implored me to wait to transition. Until after college and a career maybe. She told me horror stories of trans women she knew from the streets who were found murdered and mutilated. If she had to bury me, she told me she wouldn't forgive me.
>
> She screamed and cried about it. But I retorted that the idea of letting puberty finish the job was simply worse than death. Period.

When it's a matter of survival, when it's sex work or an unlivable life, what do you choose? And at what cost? Luckily, Alyssa is still with us, a blessing every day.

I feel so lucky to have met Crystal Kimewon through another Canadian sex worker; so often First Nations and Indigenous women are left out of communal conversations around sex work and rights because ongoing imperialism and settler colonialism have created a very different reality for our Indigenous comrades, one in which sex work is very often unwanted sexual exploitation, compounding existing trauma. Crystal generously agreed to talk to me for over an hour, about her youth in the Canadian child welfare system, which is only now beginning to redress the history of removal of First Nations children from their families, which goes back to at least the mid-nineteenth century; about how she came to social work and organizing for sex workers' and Indigenous women's rights; and about what she wants to see going forward from white women in the sex workers' rights movement.

Aubrey is the only non-sex worker contributor in this collection; she's a social worker who ran a popular (within social work student circles) blog about graduate school for social work and then about her early career as a social worker working with youth in the foster system. One day she sent me a letter detailing how my breakdown of the exploitation of dancers in strip clubs had enabled her to connect with one of her kiddos in a way she'd never been able to before, allowing the girl to draw a connection between the exploitation of dancers by club management and the series of predatory men in her life. Aubrey, wise to the ways of contrary teenagers, didn't do the usual hand-wringing about how bad it is to be a stripper. Instead, she ran through the math I had shared on my own blog when I was suing my club, the absurd fee structure that keeps club owners rich and dancers beginning their shifts in debt, sometimes leaving with a bag and sometimes leaving further in debt. We don't know how the girl in Aubrey's letter is doing—she's aged out of the system by now—but she could be many of us, starting life without social, financial, or educational capital, but thanks to Aubrey, she begins with a lens through which to see the power dynamics of the sex industry (and her relationships) more clearly than many of us start with.

Moving from Aubrey's explanation of how the club works, I ask, "What's your price?" in "Intimate Labor," trying to push non-sex workers to imaginatively engage with sex work from a new angle: as providers of sexual services rather than consumers or judgy bystanders. I ask the same questions over and over, repeatedly failing to generate any kind of engagement other than scandalized delight. How do we conceive of money, value, and the value of different kinds of labor? What kinds of activities generate respect? Which generate money, but no respect at all? Do respect and value levels correspond to tangible benefits produced by our labor? If labor is unseen, can it be known and valued? Sweat and labor render some products more valuable, and others less: like with a ballet dancer, no one wants to see the effort going into our production of sexy affection.

And continuing on the theme of labor, Susan Shepard takes a frank look at why strippers, on the surface prime candidates to push for labor rights, somehow never successfully manage to pull it off. In a system in which all work is bad and all workers are exploited, with workers' rights increasingly gutted across the board, there are no great options or perfect answers. She drives this home: "Once again, sing it with me: How well a dancer is treated isn't a consequence of worker status. It's a consequence of whether or not the club owner is a greedy dickhead."

We end with Dee Lucas and "Metatopia," her argument for the necessity of hope and the radical imagination in helping us to create the better world we all deserve. I have known Dee for years, through periods of depression as well as delight, and it's often been Dee's thinking that has offered me a roadmap out of depression. It's often hard to hold hope and imagine a future less bleak than our present, but Dee compels us to go past the dreams that comfort us in an increasingly dismal reality, demanding that we

> Understand that "imagination" is not some miraculous quality of children's books or simply an attractive fantasy theme. Imagination is conception; it's where consciousness models and prepares for possible outcomes. Imagination is the ability to render in the mind an image of immaterial reality! In our minds, we can create that which does not yet exist. thus do all our works, stories, and inventions arise "from nothing."

Dee reminds us that imaginative play is a tool for learning as well as a way to rest and relax, and she offers us what she calls "Metatopia":

> Metatopia is not defined by an enforced aesthetic, nor is it derivative of social anxieties. Rather, it is defined by being a constructive social fantasy done with the intent of influencing the real world to create societies where equality, liberation, and joy are fundamental aims.

If we have a moral obligation to leave this world a more just and beautiful place than we found it—and, like Dee, I personally believe that we do—we cannot just live through this while self-soothing the despair. We have to imagine our way to the future we deserve.

The pieces in this book run the gamut from academic examinations of labor exploitation and commentary on historians to first-person narratives, literary studies, and interviews. Each contributor is doing more than surviving—in their own ways, each person in this book is working to make sense of the reality we've been given and find a way to thrive outside of the confines of the circumstances we were born into, creating new futures and possibilities and rejecting the toxic competition and resource extraction cycle of capitalism through sex work, art, writing, and building communities of care. I hope they can act as comfort and a reminder of things I frequently need to remember myself: You are not alone. And there is hope.

Selected Further Reading

On the history of human trafficking and related panics in the United States:
Ditmore, Melissa. *Unbroken Chains*. Boston: Beacon Press, 2023.

On trafficking stats:
Gallagher, Anne. "The Global Slavery Index Is Based on Flawed Data—Why Does No One Say So?" *Guardian*, November 28, 2014. https://www.theguardian.com/global-development/poverty-matters/2014/nov/28/global-slavery-index-walk-free-human-trafficking-anne-gallagher.
Kessler, Glenn. "Why You Should Be Wary of Statistics on Modern Day Slavery and Trafficking." *Washington Post*, April 24, 2015. https://www.washingtonpost.com/news/fact-checker/wp/2015/04/24/why-you-should-be-wary-of-statistics-on-modern-slavery-and-trafficking.

On the creation of the twenty-first-century War on Trafficking:
Doezema, Jo. *Sex Slaves and Discourse Masters*. New York: Zed Books, 2010.
Hobbes, Michael, and Sarah Marshall. "Human Trafficking." *You're Wrong About* (podcast), November 25, 2019. Mike tells Sarah how NGOs, activists, and George W. Bush resurrected the "stranger danger" panic for the modern era. Digressions include "reply all," muffins, and Yelp for massage parlors.
Kempadoo, Kamala, with Jyoti Sanghera and Bandana Pattanaik. *Trafficking and Prostitution Reconsidered: New Perspectives on Migration, Sex Work, and Human Rights*. Boulder, CO: Paradigm, 2005.
Mac, Juno, and Molly Smith. *Revolting Prostitutes*. London: Verso, 2018.

On domestic minor sex trafficking:
Lutnick, Alex. *Domestic Minor Sex Trafficking*. New York: Columbia University Press, 2016.
Showden, Carisa R., and Samantha Majic. *Youth Who Trade Sex in the US: Intersectionality, Agency, and Vulnerability*. Philadelphia: Temple University Press, 2018.

Notes

1 J.R. Ujifusa, "Presentation before City Club of Portland," City Club of Portland January Meeting, Kell's Irish Pub, Portland, Oregon, Panel on Trafficking, January 2015.
2 SESTA/FOSTA, the Stop Enabling Sex Traffickers Act/Fight Online Sex Trafficking Act in the Senate and House respectively, weakened Section 230

of the Communications Decency Act, the 1996 US act that protected Internet services from being held liable for the actions or speech of their users. Section 230 specifically dealt with civil law and does not apply to criminal law or violations of criminal law.

3   George Bush, "Address to the United Nations General Assembly," United Nations, September 23, 2003, https://www.un.org/webcast/ga/58/statements/usaeng030923.htm.

4   "2019 Trafficking in Persons Report: United States," United States Department of State, Office to Monitor and Combat Trafficking in Persons, https://www.state.gov/reports/2019-trafficking-in-persons-report-2/united-states.

5   "2019 Trafficking in Persons Report: United States."

6   "The Typology of Modern Slavery: Defining Sex and Labor Trafficking in the United States," Polaris, March 2017, https://polarisproject.org/sites/default/files/Polaris-Typology-of-Modern-Slavery.pdf.

7   Carisa R. Showden and Samantha Majic, *Youth Who Trade Sex in the US: Intersectionality, Agency, and Vulnerability* (Philadelphia: Temple University Press, 2018), 80–81.

8   Showden and Majic, *Youth Who Trade Sex in the US*, 82.

9   Showden and Majic, *Youth Who Trade Sex in the US*, 87.

10   Hallie Rubenfeld, *The Covent Garden Ladies* (London: Black Swan, 2020); Luise White, *The Comforts of Home* (Chicago: University of Chicago Press, 1990)

Life at the Margins: A Roadmap for the Revolution

Leila Raven

The question regularly resurfaces in leftist circles: "Will sex work exist after the revolution?" Maybe, and maybe not. Regardless of the answer to that question, two things remain true: people who trade sex for resources deserve to live free from state violence right now, and people trading sex by choice, circumstance, or coercion know best about what they need to be safe. Those of us who have traded sex to survive also have insights we can offer on what it might take to make a revolution. Our lessons about care work from surviving in the margins offer a roadmap.

Oppressive hierarchies are baked into the way that capitalist culture teaches us to structure our society, our schools, and, most disconcertingly, our families. Many young people are taught that respect means obedience and that it is owed to people who are older, stronger, or in positions of authority. The agency and autonomy of young people is often invalidated in a way that contradicts many of the lessons we teach about healthy relationships within the movement to end violence.

The work of untangling ourselves from oppressive systems starts here and now. The model we need to transform our society does not lie within oppressive structures like the patriarchal nuclear family. Instead, we have to look to the margins, where Black, disabled, trans, and queer people in the sex trades are building relationships and networks of kinship that subvert oppressive norms. As Saidiya Hartman writes in her 2019 book *Wayward Lives, Beautiful Experiments*, "The mutuality and creativity necessary to sustain living in the context of intermittent wages, controlled depletion, economic exclusion, coercion, and anti-black violence often bordered on the extralegal and criminal." People who live at the margins create new norms out of necessity. Our survival strategies offer a roadmap for resistance against oppression and a model for living in the world we want to create.

The dominant culture criticizes, stigmatizes, and even criminal-izes people like us who choose alternative family structures and ways of making a living. "You're her mother, not her friend," I've been told. And what if I am her friend? What if I have let go of any desire to control or dominate the child I'm raising, and what if I believe a good friend is a good caregiver who does everything in their power to listen and ensure that those in their care are heard and affirmed, are kept safe, and are supported in being accountable to their values and their community? What if I have accepted that the child in my care is not my property, that I do not own or control her?

You don't read about caregivers like us in most parenting books. We are street kids who have become caregivers. We were separated from those who birthed us by state violence, whether by police brutality, incarceration, harmful immigration policies, or intervention by the family policing system. In some way or ways, the connection to our blood relationships has been disrupted, and we learned new ways of cultivating relationships with each other, surviving through some combination of mutual aid and criminalized labor. Some of us worried that we could never become parents or caregivers because of the trauma, abuse, and neglect that we experienced. But now we know: our alternative lifestyles are not signs of our brokenness but rather signs of our survival against all odds, symbols of our resistance and our ability to envision a world where we all take collective responsibility for the safety and well-being of our whole communities, where we see caregiving for each other not as a burden but as a given, and where we understand respect for the consent and autonomy of others as a framework for building our relationships.

We've had the chance to unburden ourselves of the oppressive beliefs that children are property, that families are nuclear, and that these norms can be coerced through the threat of punishment. Our lack of experience in the nuclear family isn't a source of shame, but a resource.

Our alternative modes of surviving and caring for each other show up in many communities navigating oppression, for whom the cookie-cutter mold of the nuclear family structure wasn't built. As trans and queer people, and especially as people of color, who have experienced family rejection and homelessness, we forge networks of kinship rooted not in blood relations but in mutual respect, empathy, kindness, and care.

Power doesn't have to be expressed by dominating others and upholding oppressive hierarchies. It can be expressed by listening, learning, and leveraging our positions to support and amplify the voices of others. We have to cede power in order to build up young people's capacity to care for themselves and each other.

We are much more powerful that way.

Adrie Rose

Do you remember the first time you learned that selling sex or performing sexy was a way to make money?
I didn't understand what selling sex was when I was dabbling in sugaring, but my mother has always told me relationships should be more than momentarily beneficial. I understood the power differential in hetero relationships very early in life. It wasn't until I moved out on my own, in my early twenties, that I genuinely understood what that meant. I matched with a guy on Tinder who offered me four hundred dollars for a blow job. I thought it was a joke, so I didn't respond, but then he offered more money and he offered to pay for my Uber. It was the first time I ever saw the inside of the Miami Yacht Club, and it paid more than half of my rent.

Did you know it would be something that you would do for income at that point?
Oddly enough, I never thought twice about it. BackPage and Craigslist personals were still ubiquitous at the time, so it was simple enough to find ads that I liked and adapt them to my style.

There was absolutely a period of trial and error. I tried to recreate my initial Tinder success on other dating apps and ended up matching

Self-Portrait, by Adrie Rose

with a guy who was very obviously a pimp, but I was young and stupid. I lost a bank account and ended up having to talk to the cops because this man was sleeping in his car outside of my apartment, threatening my neighbors or any man on the sidewalk. Of course, the cops did nothing (except try to extort me in exchange for them doing their jobs), but it worked itself out.

Aside from that situation, I never dealt with anything particularly egregious. Learning to deal with time wasters and slobbyists was probably the most time-consuming part. That, and learning to manage my time. Once I started treating it like a business, studying other people's ads, getting separate devices strictly for work, and being smarter about screening and my own safety, it got a lot easier.

When did you decide to trade sex/ualized services?
As I was leaving the Tinder match's apartment with six hundred dollars in cash.

Did you first start working in a space or field where there were other sex workers around, or did you work in isolation? What was that like?
I worked alone for the first few months. Once I realized there was a community on Tumblr, I started making friends with people in my area. There's safety in numbers (to an extent), so I always preferred to work with others. In a larger city, working with others also affords you greater opportunities for consistent income, because someone always knows someone that's having a party.

Did you start out in a line of sex work you thought you would want to continue in, or were you treading water and learning with a plan to change it up? Can you talk about why?
I never considered anything else, because I always knew this wasn't my long-term career. I wanted to go back to school, I wanted to teach, and I didn't want my face to forever be tied to sex work, so I never considered porn or anything online.

What are some songs that were popular or that you loved when you first started doing sex work?
I was in Miami, so I listened to a lot of reggaeton, because it was everywhere.

How has sex work—the way you do it, the way you think it's perceived and understood by outsiders, and the community of sex workers you know (if any)—changed since you started?

I don't know if the perception has changed much in the last eight or nine years. I think the conversation is changing, but I think people are still largely, and willfully, ignorant of what sex work is and looks like. Part of that is really good propaganda on the part of certain interest groups and their celebrity mouthpieces, but part of that is also a societal urge to delegitimize traditionally feminized labor.

What music do you listen to to get pumped for work?

Depends on the day. I have a playlist for every occasion, so sometimes it's metal, sometimes it's disco, sometimes it's '80s pop, or sometimes it's R & B/soul from the '70s and '80s.

What do you do to relax after a bad shift or client?

I guess it's both a blessing and a curse that I've always been able to immediately compartmentalize client experiences. I don't think about them once they're over. Bad clients are no different for me. Once it's over and I have my money, I cease thinking about them. If they're particularly bad, I'll do the usual bad-date routine of uploading the number and my experience to Client Eye, but that's it.

Do you remember your first big money purchase with sex work money? What was it? How did you feel?

Rent, I think? And I think I paid off my cell phone. It was a Samsung Note 5, and I was overjoyed because it was the first phone I owned outright.

Do you feel like having done sex work has given you certain skills that are useful in your day-to-day or non-swing life that others don't have? What are some of them? Are there disadvantages from sex work that also come up? If there are, will you elaborate on them?

I don't know if I'd consider it a skill, but I have learned to trust my instincts immediately and without question. If it looks like a cop or sounds like a cop, I don't ask questions. I just block and move along. If it feels like a pimp, instant block. Aside from that, being able to clock a time-waster or a bullshit artist is something that I've had to perfect.

What do you think would make sex workers' lives better or easier or safer (or all three)?
Decriminalization. Comprehensive sex ed that includes definitions of consent. For people to mind their business.

Do you feel like you're a part of a larger community of sex workers? In person or on the Internet?
Yes and no. The Internet has been amazing for building a community of organizers and activists that I consider my friends. But I don't consider many sex workers to be my community, because a lot of them are tied to racist, classist, and capitalist values that I find to be violent and/or antithetical to my survival.

Those people are not my community.

How do you see power dynamics play out in your community? What kind of workers are valued by other sex workers around you, and what kind of work is most valued?
I don't think it's industry specific. White women, especially thin, cis white women, get away with literal murder. All of the "-isms" that play out in the larger society play out in the microcosm that is the sex industry. White women are platformed, deified, and revered as the figureheads of the sex trade, full stop, and this happens regardless of hierarchal positions. I could talk about this endlessly, and I have written about it, but look at the ways non-sex-trading white women are given a voice in the community over Black and brown sex workers, especially those who are disabled and/or migrants. Beyond that, there is definitely a trend of platforming college-educated women who peddle a narrative of empowerment and financial success.

Do you feel involved in sex worker activism or organizing? Do you want to be?
Very marginally. I hesitate to ever call myself an activist or an organizer. I'm just loud and privileged because I'm occupying academic spaces; that doesn't make me an activist. I believe in sharing information and resources with the most marginalized people, and I don't believe in catering to white ignorance. People have chosen to listen to me because of that. I'm ambivalent.

What kind of organizing goals are prioritized by the sex workers around you?
I make it a point to surround myself with people who care about decriminalization, decarceration, abolition, and redistribution of wealth and resources.

What do you think are barriers to achieving those goals?
Willful ignorance, interest groups with federal funding and celebrity spokespeople, media creators and gatekeepers who don't want to tell stories unrelated to trauma porn or empowerment narratives.

How are you coping with our current reality?
I'm asthmatic, so forced isolation takes on a deeper meaning during a global health crisis, but I'm greatly enjoying the excuse to focus on things that bring me joy and keep me fed as opposed to things that just make me money.

The Monotony of Sex Work

Sarah

A sex worker friend and I were having a conversation about things out in the world that we instantly associate with work. She looked at me a little bit funny when I said my first thought was Dr. Phil. I have spent so many hours waiting around in dead day shifts in dingy brothels watching *Dr. Phil* or *Dr. Oz* or any of those bloody daytime shows that I think they'll always remind me of sex work. I have as many funny stories as the next person, but today I want to talk about monotony.

I think of the boredom of that same interaction every time the phone rings: the inevitable paraphrase of "I've never been with a woman like you before," of explaining for the twelve-hundredth time the same things they could have read in the damn ad, of trying to make sure they get that they have to actually book a time and show up and that they've read my rates, of being on guard for the familiar signs that someone is wasting my time, of being talked down to because my body can't do things that a post-transition trans woman's body is unlikely to do easily.

I think of how often those bookings follow the same script. My clientele don't want emotional labor in the form of anything resembling normal social interaction: they want emotional labor in the form of subtle reassurance that whatever it is that they particularly want to do with somebody else's penis makes them not gay. I am so beyond bored of having to reassure men that they're not gay for being attracted to women, usually based on what they've seen in a type of porn directed at and made for straight men. I am so tired of convincing them that the high-drama crisis of sexuality playing out in their mind at that particular moment is basically the same as every other client who ever came before them and that it doesn't necessarily make them anything. I am not the world's best conversationalist, but having to put in serious effort to get more than the barest of small talk out of men who are so totally preoccupied with freaking out that they're attracted to *you* is so utterly fucking boring. I am over having to regurgitate an emotional ego massage that never gets any deeper than, "Am I *gaaaaaaaay*?"

I think of the regular anxiety that comes with not knowing when you'll next have money coming in because your city is in recession and that fact is driving workers into the industry as fast as it is driving paying clients out of it. I think of the panic of watching the pantry and the fridge get barer and barer in the bad weeks, and of the anxiety of the judgment calls you have to make when you get the client equivalent of dregs in those situations—not even "Is this someone I want to see?" or "Is this person going to be a dick?" but "Is there even money at the end of dealing with this particular load of bullshit?"

I think of how civilians who think of themselves as "sex positive" or "sex negative" never comprehend this side of the industry. Whether they think we're having a lot of enthusiastic, empowering sex, or whether they think we've got clients lined up around the block while we're visibly unenthusiastic, these things are so far from the reality. Quitting brothel work when that side of the industry went to hell at least gave me the sweet, sweet blessing of never, ever having to watch *Dr. Phil* again, but sex work still involves way too much time on social media or on Netflix waiting for clients, who when they do come will more often than not be about as monotonous.

This is the side of sex work that doesn't make for glamorous dramatizations or pity porn or the entire badly-written-former-sex-worker-memoir genre, but it is as much a part of it. There will always be the funny stories and the gross stories and the irrepressible sisterhood with other workers, but fuck, I expect I will always remember the fucking monotony too.

A gross story: A few weeks into my time in the industry, I had a booking that gave me the very sudden realization that sex work was not, in fact, always going to be particularly sexy. I was pulling a late-night brothel shift with a drag queen who made no secret of the fact she had far broader boundaries with clients than my then-quite-vanilla self and wasn't fazed by much, and we were the only two people on shift when a client walked in.

She saw his face on the CCTV, immediately balked, and refused to intro him because he was too gross. I quite wisely got the picture that this was not a good sign, but I felt obliged to intro as the new girl and the only one on and, despite being as intentionally dismal as possible in that intro, was chosen. And boy, she was not wrong. I found myself in a room with a beyond morbidly obese man, chest and back a morass of sores and hair, who had not dried between his rolls of fat, who was about as physically grotesque as I could imaginably find the words to describe.

And if this story had just been about the time I saw a ferociously fugly client, that would be one thing. Oh no. This man had—keeping in mind everything I've just described—the biggest Casanova complex I've ever seen in a client. He was completely and utterly convinced that he was God's gift to women and proceeded to detail, in very great depth, how every hooker he'd ever seen was madly in love with him. I got to hear about all his high-drama high jinks that read to him as some sort of wonderful love affairs but read, uh, quite differently to someone with things like perspective and boundaries.

This was not helped by the brothel receptionist's always-eclectic take on what to pipe into the rooms. They have some terrible radio show called "Love Songs, Dedications, and Requests" that plays on airplanes here, and for some reason this was playing in the room this entire time. Vomitous public declarations and bad love songs don't please my ears at the best of times, but especially not while trying to find the dick of the world's most repulsive client. I subsequently discovered that the reason the music finally stopped was because the drag queen had lost patience with that as a soundtrack to her giving head to another random dude, stormed out to reception mid-booking half-starkers, and changed the station herself.

I remember spending that booking thinking, "Well, at least I know that as long as I work I will never deal with a more repulsive client." More than two years later, while one lecherous, toothless ninety-year-old might have given him a run for his money, that still holds true. And I'm still friends with that drag queen, and we still remember that client who we bonded over our mutual disgust for.

Art by Beyondeep

Sage

Do you remember the first time you learned that selling sex or performing sexy was a way to make money?
Yes.

How did you find out, and what was your immediate reaction?
When I was eighteen years old, I went to a strip club in Indiana called Industrial Strip. That was the first time I had ever seen a stripper and the first time I learned how it all worked. I thought they were gorgeous. I thought the things they could do were so cool. That was the first time that people who were that beautiful and strong noticed me and were kind to me. They even invited me back to work there if I wanted. I was in love.

Did you know it would be something that you would do for income at that point?
No.

When did you decide to trade sex/ualized services?
Four years after that first time in a strip club, when I graduated from college, I decided to strip until I could find a solid job in my field of study.

Did you first start working in a space or field where there were other sex workers around, or did you work in isolation? What was that like?
I worked in a small lounge with other strippers there. They were all really nice and helpful to me.

Did you start out in a line of sex work you thought you would want to continue in, or were you treading water and learning with a plan to change it up? Club jumping counts here. Can you talk about why?
When I first started, I went into it thinking it would be temporary, because that's how I was told college works. You get your four-year degree and then someone scoops you up for work. Upon realizing that was a big lie and work that could actually sustain you is pretty rare, I got comfortable with being a stripper. I didn't dance with an exit plan. Dancing *was* the exit plan. When I got better at dancing, I wanted to try out different clubs, because the owners of my first club were racist. I went to a larger, more popular club. Management there was colorist. I left there and finally found a place where I felt the safest. That was a gown club that had been rebuilt in 2018.

What are some songs that were popular or that you loved when you first started doing sex work?
Songs I loved:
 "I Love You"–Lido
 "Where Are Ü Now"–Jack Ü, Skrillex, Diplo, Justin Bieber
 "Trndsttr"–Black Coast
 "Eyes on Fire"–Blue Foundation, Zeds Dead
 "One Time"–Marian Hill
 "Feds Watching"–2 Chainz
 "Choose Me"–Xilent
 "Wildfire"–SBTRKT

Songs that were popular:
 "Plastic Bag"–Drake Future
 "Diamonds Dancing"–Drake Future
 "Often"–The Weeknd
 "No Problem"–Chance the Rapper
 "Sex with Me"–Rihanna
 "679"–Fetty Wap
 "Right Hand"–Drake

How has sex work—the way you do it, the way you think it's perceived and understood by outsiders, and the community of sex workers you know (if any)—changed since you started?

I love it more than I did going into it, which was already a lot. I don't appreciate the warring factions of our community or the racism, but I still enjoy being able to express myself and support myself in this way.

Outsiders used to hate and dehumanize us by way of insult and degradation. Now they hate and dehumanize us by way of fetishization, appropriation, and voyeurism (*Hustlers*, *P-Valley*, pole classes, "twerk" classes, "sensual stretch" classes, "exotic" pole, etc.). I'm not a fan of that. I would very much like it to stop.

Do you feel like you're a part of a larger community of sex workers? In person or on the Internet?

No, I don't feel a strong sense of community. I've always worked alone and never danced consistently enough to have a "home club" or clique. I'm always willing to help out other sex workers in person or online, but I kinda do my own thing outside of that.

How do you see power dynamics play out in your community? What kind of workers are valued by other sex workers around you, and what kind of work is most valued?

From my observation, it seems like the less physical contact you make with people, the more "valuable" your work is within the sex worker community. People don't seem to respect full-service sex workers at all, and then other full-service workers discriminate against each other based on whether they travel, how much they charge, what boundaries they have, etc. Very weird. Then sugar babies are seen as a step up from that because of only having one client for a long time and the image of luxury projected out there of them. Strippers either tie for that same spot as sugar babies or they are perceived as slightly above them, because no sex acts are being performed unless a person chooses to do extras. Then other strippers shame the ones who do extras. Above strippers are cam models, because there's no physical contact required and I guess it's perceived as "cleaner" than all the other forms of sex work. Then at the peak of sophistication and respect is burlesque dancers, or, as I like to call them, strippers dipped in rhinestones. They do the exact same thing strippers and cam models do, but because they do it *sloooowly* and to jazz piano, that somehow makes them better than *all* of us. I still haven't figured out the logic behind that one. A lot of them don't even do any cool tricks or anything. And a lot of them don't even classify themselves as sex workers, even though that's exactly what they're doing. Ridiculous.

Do you feel involved in sex worker activism or organizing? Do you want to be?
I am quietly working in the background. I monitor legislation and donate to causes when I have the resources. I also dance for sex worker charity events whenever they're presented to me.

What kind of organizing goals are prioritized by the sex workers around you?
In DC, the focus is the effort to decriminalize sex work and establish mutual aid funds for sex workers' food, shelter, legal battles, etc.

Regardless of whether you're involved in activism or organizing, what do you see as important goals for us to work toward?
Removing as much harmful legislation and stigma as we possibly can. Then reinstating our rights to privacy.

What do you think are barriers to achieving those goals?
SESTA/FOSTA, social stigma fueled by patriarchal and capitalist teaching, straight-up jealousy and hatred.

How are you coping with our current reality?
Honestly? I'm not.

What would you like to see from white sex workers moving forward? Individually and/or as a community and/or as organizers?
I need them to use their privilege to protect sex workers of color, especially Black sex workers, because they are valued the least in our industry. Use their privilege to give sex workers of color a platform. I also need them to understand that not every conversation is for them. Allow people of color to claim and protect their contributions to this industry that are specific to their culture. Sometimes gatekeeping is necessary and it's okay.

White Supremacy in Organizing

Domino Rey

Over the years at various parties, square friends of friends would ask me what it was like to be a stripper. They often assumed I made thousands of dollars a night, worked only when I wanted to, drove a luxury car, and was swimming in designer clothes, shoes, and handbags. When I told them sometimes on truly awful nights I'd leave owing the house money, they'd look at me, confused. "Owe money?" they'd ask.

"Yeah, we pay to work. The fee depends on the time and day. We have to pay even if there's nobody in the club, if they aren't tipping, if we get robbed, no matter what. Sometimes they keep rolling over the debts week to week till you have no hope of paying it off."

Some guys flat out didn't believe me when I told them this. "How is it possible, in America, in the 2000s, people pay to work?" one mused aloud.

I snorted. "Try being a woman. Try being not white. Try being poor. Try having so little power that any sort of resistance to policies at work means potentially being out of a job, which isn't an option when you have rent and bills due and no savings."

He considered, then shook his head. "I still can't believe it."

And that's exactly why club management continues to get away with it: because sometimes, despite how egregious the exploitation is, the

Parking, by Scarlett

workers are so used to mistreatment—and know no alternatives—that the situation becomes normal. Because of who is abused, their place in society, their power and influence (or lack thereof), their race, and other intersections ... nothing ever changes. There are too many obstacles to overcome, with the onus of change on marginalized workers with a virtually nonexistent grasp on job security, sometimes living hand to mouth, one late payment away from eviction, losing custody of children, or having to withdraw from school. Confronting these abuses would require a reckoning with white supremacy, capitalism, our values, how we determine community, how we treat women, how we view sex and women's ownership of their own sexuality and the commodification of it, and a myriad of other topics usually off-limits to discussion in our society. It would also potentially mean losing one's job, getting black-listed from chains of clubs (sometimes the only ones in the vicinity of the dancer), and becoming alienated from coworkers.

What's even more frustrating is that dancers continue to replicate these greater systems of harm and hierarchy within the club, and that also makes it so hard to name and dismantle, because, like in the world at large, those who benefit the most from our skewed system often have that same power and replicate the same systems of harm at work. Because the club encourages the ruthless, cutthroat dynamics of capitalism and often pits dancers against one another, our ties among one another are often tenuous at best—and often openly contentious. The interests of the dancers who reap the most benefits (having the most desirable shifts, the favor of management, etc.) are often in opposition to the interests of the dancers who stand to gain the most, and a lot of privileged dancers simply aren't willing to give up perks and unearned advantages in the name of dancer unity.

Despite the fact that the idea of sex work as work has fully entered the mainstream, and that major cities across the US are considering the decriminalization of prostitution,[1] relatively few people are aware of the exploitation that occurs in the legal arenas of sex work, like the strip club: namely, how strippers are forced to pay the club to be able to work, calling the mandatory payment of anywhere from ten to three hundred dollars "house fees"; the expectation of tipping out house moms, DJs, bouncers, valets, VIP hosts, and sometimes even management; and the fines for missed shifts, not fully disrobing on stage, not complying with dress codes—you name it, there's a fine for it.

One of the ways clubs get away with forcing dancers to pay to work is by classifying them as independent contractors rather than as employees for wage purposes. Independent contractors are supposed to be workers who are hired by an entity that performs a service that is outside the entity's main purpose of business. In a strip club, an example of this would be a plumber hired to come in to fix a leaking toilet. The workers who perform the main stated purpose of a business (e.g., strippers in a strip club) are supposed to be hired as employees, complete with all of the rights and privileges afforded therein: for example, getting paid an hourly wage and overtime; having taxes withheld from your wages; the right to disability benefits, paid leave, and sick days if working full-time; the right to organize and form a labor union; access to unemployment; and legal protections from sexual harassment and discrimination based on race, gender, and other protected statuses.

However, strip clubs have never been in the business of treating their workers fairly, and as such, they hire strippers as independent contractors, meaning that the strippers get none of the previously stated benefits. There is no recourse for federally protected statuses like race, gender, and disability and no protections against sexual harassment. Independent contractors must pay all of their own Social Security and Medicare taxes, resulting in a larger portion of wages paid to taxes, and the burden of obtaining health insurance falls on the worker. Additionally, independent contractors do not have paid sick days or leave, do not have an hourly wage or overtime, and cannot access unemployment benefits when out of work.[2]

Strippers in California were handed a win in 2019 with the passage of Assembly Bill 5 (AB5), which sought to clarify the criteria a business must use to determine whether workers are independent contractors or employees.[3] AB5 implemented the "ABC test," which uses the following criteria to determine a worker's status as an independent contractor:

a. Are free of control and direction by the hiring company (*At the strip club, this would look like not having to put oneself on the schedule and get fined for missing shifts, not having a dress code beyond complying with local decency laws, being free to dance to whatever music onstage, not having to stay for a minimum amount of time per shift, and not having to pay house fees.*)

b. Perform work outside the usual course of business of the hiring entity (*Going back to the example of a plumber doing*

work in a strip club, strippers at a strip club are most certainly performing work within the usual course of business.)
and
c.   Are independently established in that trade, occupation, or business. *(For strippers, this looks like being able to work at multiple clubs without penalty, being able to do one-off performances as a featured dancer rather than being compelled to work regular shifts like a house girl, and being able to negotiate their own prices for dances and VIP/champagne rooms.)*[4]

In reality, how dancers fare on a nightly basis is subject to a myriad of variables beyond whether they are classified as an employee or as an independent contractor: everything from the time of year, the dancer's race and skin tone, the geographic location of the club, and local zoning laws and laws pertaining to alcohol sales (for example, in Los Angeles, alcohol sales are banned at nude clubs but allowed in topless clubs) to the target customer base of the club (for example, at "urban" clubs, most of a dancer's money comes in the form of stage tips, while at clubs that market themselves as "gentleman's clubs," there is often more money to be made in selling longer amounts of time in private rooms).

Despite all these variables that drastically impact the quality of work for strippers outside of worker classification status, around the time that AB5 was up for consideration in the California State Assembly, two other strippers and I decided to start an advocacy group in Southern California, where we all lived at the time, with the goal of raising awareness about the bill and the benefits of employee status for gig work (a term that nowadays is mostly associated with app-based platforms like ride shares and meal delivery but could also encompass the way many strippers pick up occasional shifts at the club) and advocating for strippers to form a labor union (which we believed possible under AB5 at the time; more on that later). Our goal was to help strippers across disparate clubs and areas of California get to know one another and unite for a common goal. We realized that the power of organization was only as strong as our community and our willingness to advocate for one another. We decided on a set of priorities: ending wage theft through house fees and illegal tipouts, ending sexual harassment and assault in the club by customers and staff alike, and ending racist, colorist hiring practices, as many clubs have unspoken caps for Black and brown strippers (often one) and often hire only the lightest-skinned, most European-looking ones.

I began my time with this group starry-eyed, convinced that with such lofty goals, the power of social media, and a knack for generating publicity, we could successfully pull off a labor movement the likes of which had been unseen in our industry. We had the advantage of the guidance of strippers involved in the unionization effort of the Lusty Lady in San Francisco in the late 1990s; we hoped their tactics and strategies could inform our own, and we trusted that their advice and experience would get us far. We started off strong, hosting weekly virtual events that were open forums for dancers to air their grievances with the clubs, learn more about AB5, discover what we stood to gain if we became employees, and also get to know one another.

While we started to build momentum within our community, we also started to reach out to local unions, testing the waters to see who would be willing to potentially sponsor us and mentor us as we attempted to unionize. We quickly realized that, while being avid consumers of our services, few men, no matter how left-leaning politically, wanted to publicly admit to such and support our cause. Most unions we contacted turned us down, as publicly backing strippers was too politically volatile. Some said they liked the idea of what we were doing and admired the fact that our work had many implications for non-sex-work-based gig workers who stood to gain many rights and advantages from employee status, but they didn't see how we belonged in the labor rights movement. Some even questioned our intelligence and wondered how we had enough collective smarts to pull off what we were attempting. It was disheartening, to say the least, how few people were willing to see us as fellow workers in the struggle against exploitation.

Many of us organizers also hit up our sugar daddies and tricks for help, and while they quietly sent us money to support our movement, none spoke out openly about supporting us. Many men fancy themselves open-minded and forward-thinking and "support sex workers" in that abstract, social-media-based-activism sense, in which people post one infographic and assume they have done their part. Alas, those who would take tangible steps to support fair treatment by boycotting clubs and potentially paying higher fees to come see us failed to materialize.

In late 2019, we had our first wildcat strike outside of a glossy, high-profile club in Hollywood that was known for its celebrity clientele and ostentatious money wars, in which patrons competed to see who could tip the most by "making it rain" onstage, which were edited into slick highlight reels and widely shared on social media. We figured that such a known target was the perfect starting place for our movement, because of how much attention it received on a regular basis; it turns out we were partially right. The participants of the strike turned out to be exclusively dancers from other clubs, as well as a handful of supporters from anarchist and socialist workers' rights groups. Despite the lean turnout of picketers, the strike gained a lot of media attention. I was interviewed for the local news, a Spanish-language news channel, and a communist newspaper, and more interview requests, as well as a feature on the front page of the *Los Angeles Times*, followed as a result.[5]

Our movement came on the heels of the New York City stripper strike, and the agitation from strippers on both coasts turned our efforts into national news. Despite the attention of the media, we had a dearth of strippers locally supporting us—it turns out, when your livelihood is on the line and even if you desperately want better working conditions, almost nobody is willing to go without a night's pay to send a message to management without the backing of a union, nor are they willing to risk being fired to join a picket line or speak up in the dressing room. This type of ask highlighted the stark divide in the stripper community: some of the strippers involved passionately believed in the cause and desperately wanted better working conditions, but their positions at elite, high-earning clubs were so tenuous that they felt they couldn't risk taking a stand.

Meanwhile, privileged dancers who made considerably more and had job security due to their relationships with management, their race, and other factors were unwilling to release the vice grip they had on unfair advantages they enjoyed in the name of protecting the most vulnerable in the workforce. Some even went as far as to perceive our movement as a threat, and they became informants for management, infiltrating our meetings and passing along talking points to the club staff. The media's coverage and our online support prompted a backlash from management at many clubs, who told their dancers in no uncertain terms that posting our group's graphics on their social media pages or speaking about unfair conditions or our group at work would lead to termination, even though it's illegal to fire workers engaged in active unionization campaigns.

These were blows to my morale, but I believed in this cause so passionately, had devoted so much time and energy into learning about labor laws, and had worked so hard to break this information down in accessible ways on social media that I was determined to keep going. What finally broke me was dynamics within the group: we were not immune to the systems of harm we had all been indoctrinated into by society, and in the end it was racial tension and imbalanced power dynamics that ultimately broke up the founding members. It started with me and another member noticing that our own group was not immune to the disease of the most privileged being unwilling to give up being centered, being comfortable, and being in control of the narrative. When we noticed that more effort was being put into lip service about diversity, inclusion, and equity rather than into implementing change based around those ideas, we decided we needed to speak up. The meeting we called went disastrously and led to attempts to intimidate and silence based on perceived personal slights. The situation then devolved into harassment, as well as public coddling of white supremacist commenters on our social media page while ignoring valid criticism from Black and brown strippers. At that point I left, as I was unwilling to put my name and integrity on a group unwilling to confront our own complicity in perpetuating unjust systems.

After I left, working conditions continued to deteriorate for workers across the board in California. In the wake of AB5 came Prop 22, a ballot initiative sponsored by ride-share companies that would carve an exemption out for their drivers, under the premise that employee protections were unnecessary and that the companies themselves could come up with alternatives for minimum income protections and health insurance for workers that were market-based.[6] The proposition passed, due largely to a massive misinformation campaign waged by the companies, scare tactics,[7] and underhanded moves like forcing app users to wade through a pop-up screen that wasn't obviously dismissible and that automatically sent a message to legislators in favor of Prop 22 whenever they opened the app to hail a ride.[8] Many strip clubs pursued similar tactics, putting letters in favor of exemptions for strippers into hiring packets and coercing strippers into signing them when onboarding at the clubs, without fully explaining what they were and what they intended to do with those signatures.

The result of Prop 22 was higher prices for app users, lower wages for workers, functionally ineffective health-care offerings, and frustration from workers and consumers alike.[9] Conditions shaped up similarly at the clubs, where the clubs pushed through a whole slew of even more unfavorable and exploitative working conditions, like taking a larger share of dance sales, making more onerous scheduling demands, and even finding ways to not have to pay workers minimum wage by deducting excessive amounts of Medicare and Social Security from strippers' paychecks (to the point where the strippers often received no base pay at all, only dance sales commissions), all while conveniently blaming these new practices on AB5.[10]

Unsurprisingly, these new, worse working conditions prompted a backlash against employee status at California strip clubs. Many strippers blamed the new measures on AB5, and the clubs were happy to have such a convenient scapegoat. Then came the additional pain of the COVID-19 pandemic, and many clubs across California shut their doors to comply with stay-at-home orders, leaving strippers without any income and no hope of receiving unemployment due to their independent-contractor status. While the pandemic rages on, many clubs have reopened, and, having been out of work for months, strippers are more desperate than ever to come back to making any sort of income at all, regardless of how terrible the conditions are at a club. There has been some organizing to create an exemption from the law, much like Prop 22, but recently a judge in California found Prop 22 unconstitutional, as its primary aim was to prevent workers from obtaining fair workplace conditions and standards as determined by the legislature.[11] At the time of this writing, I learned that AB5 doesn't allow workers in California to join unions, as that is legislated nationally by the National Labor Relations Board (NLRB) and the National Labor Relations Act, and federal law supersedes state regulations.[12] Tragically, the NLRB, whose power is traditionally to protect workers and oversee unionizing campaigns and elections, was gutted by the Trump administration. In an unprecedented set of reforms, Trump-appointed regulators have weakened long-standing protections and now take the most pro-business, antiworker stance in recent history.[13]

Trump's reformation of the NLRB into a corporate-friendly, anti-worker entity, along with the potential gubernatorial recall in California, leaves prospects bleak for all workers, but especially the most marginalized. While we know that white supremacist, capitalist, misogynistic institutions were designed to fail and punish workers like strippers, we also know that all we have is each other. In order for any meaningful change in our working conditions to happen, we have to stand together and unify around common goals. The most privileged workers must be willing to stand with the most marginalized among us and get familiar with getting uncomfortable, question systems that unfairly distribute power, and be willing to sacrifice unearned benefits in the name of protecting the most vulnerable to abuse. If we allow white supremacist, capitalist patriarchy to continue to divide us, we will all go down on this rapidly sinking ship. While it's also imperative for other industries to welcome us into organizing spaces and recognize us as workers in solidarity for better working conditions, living wages, and an end to exploitation, if we strippers continue to place the responsibility of improving working conditions on the individual, and then blame each other for the failings of the system and continue to chalk up exploitation as simply being a poor hustler, we ignore the larger, deliberate forces that shape our circumstances. Time and time again, organizers (who are often white, financially secure, and have other jobs and backup plans) have shown they're willing to do just that if they can center themselves as #girlbosses who can conquer all through their powers of stripper persuasion. It's time to squash this narrative once and for all, center the historically silenced voices, and put ego aside to improve conditions for everyone.

Notes

1   Jasmine Garsd, "Should Sex Work Be Decriminalized? Some Activists Say It's Time," *All Things Considered* (transcript), NPR, March 22, 2019, https://www.npr.org/2019/03/22/705354179/should-sex-work-be-decriminalized-some-activists-say-its-time.

2   Celine McNicholas and Margaret Poydock, "How California's AB5 Protects Workers from Misclassification," *Economic Policy Institute*, November 14, 2019, https://www.epi.org/publication/how-californias-ab5-protects-workers-from-misclassification.

3   Julia Wick, "Newsletter: California Rewrites the Rules of Employment," *Los Angeles Times*, September 12, 2019, https://www.latimes.com/california/story/2019-09-12/ab-5-future-employment-essential-california.

4   McNicholas and Poydock, "How California's AB5 Protects Workers from Misclassification."

5   "Hollywood Strippers Seeking Fair Wages, End to Alleged Sexual Harassment and Assault," *CBS Los Angeles*, February 22, 2019, https://losangeles.cbslocal.com/2019/02/22/strippers-strike-hollywood; Margot Roosevelt, "Are You an Employee or a Contractor? Carpenters, Strippers and Dog Walkers Now Face

That Question," *Los Angeles Times*, February 23, 2019, https://www.latimes.com/business/la-fi-dynamex-contractors-20190223-story.html.

6   Kari Paul, "Prop 22 Explained: How California Voters Could Upend the Gig Economy," *Guardian*, October 15, 2020, https://www.theguardian.com/us-news/2020/oct/15/proposition-22-california-ballot-measure-explained; Alexander Sammon, "Prop 22 Is Here, and It's Already Worse than Expected," *American Prospect*, January 15, 2021, https://prospect.org/labor/prop-22-is-here-already-worse-than-expected-california-gig-workers.

7   Faiz Siddiqui and Nitasha Tiku, "Uber and Lyft Used Sneaky Tactics to Avoid Making Drivers Employees in California, Voters Say. Now, They're Going National," *Washington Post*, November 17, 2020, https://www.washingtonpost.com/technology/2020/11/17/uber-lyft-prop22-misinformation.

8   Suhauna Hussain, "Uber, Lyft Push Prop. 22 Message Where You Can't Escape It: Your Phone," *Los Angeles Times*, October 8, 2020, https://www.latimes.com/business/technology/story/2020-10-08/uber-lyft-novel-tactics-huge-spending-prop-22.

9   Rachel Sandler, "Every Major Gig Company Has Now Raised Prices in California after Prop. 22," *Forbes*, February 19, 2021, https://www.forbes.com/sites/rachelsandler/2021/02/19/every-major-gig-company-has-now-raised-prices-in-california-after-prop-22/?sh=2226586d2d7c.

10   Larry Buhl, "Strippers Clash over Employment Status in Dueling L.A. Protests," *KQED*, April 3, 2019, https://www.kqed.org/news/11737567/strippers-clash-over-employment-status-in-dueling-l-a-protests; Aída Chávez, "California's New Gig Economy Law Is Strengthening a Stripper-Led Labor Movement," *The Intercept*, January 24, 2020, https://theintercept.com/2020/01/24/california-labor-law-independent-contractors-strippers.

11   Michael Hiltzik, "A California Judge Pinpointed the Biggest Problem with Prop. 22—Its Greediness," *Los Angeles Times*, August 24, 2021, https://www.latimes.com/business/story/2021-08-24/proposition-22-worker-rights.

12   McNicholas and Poydock, "How California's AB5 Protects Workers from Misclassification."

13   Celine McNicholas, Margaret Poydock, and Lynn Rhinehart, "Unprecedented: The Trump NLRB's Attack on Workers' Rights," *Economic Policy Institute*, October 16, 2019, https://www.epi.org/publication/unprecedented-the-trump-nlrbs-attack-on-workers-rights.

Self-Portrait, by Camille

Camille

Do you remember the first time you learned that selling sex or performing sexy was a way to make money?
Yes, sixteen, and thank you, Tumblr! I also remember the first time I talked to my mom about sex work. Same age, kitchen setting: I said, "Mom, will you still be proud of me if I start stripping?" My mom, *not believing me*, says yes. Okay, so *boom*, she finds out when an ex rats me out to my family, and I'll never forget the night she called before I went into a new club and told me to make a million dollars.

Did you know it would be something that you would do for income at that point?
Yes.

When did you decide to trade sex/ualized services?
Only two years later, as soon as I moved out.

Did you first start working in a space or field where there were other sex workers around, or did you work in isolation? What was that like?
I attempted to start in clubs, but there's so much to the industry in the South, so I first started camming. I was stripping within the next two years.

Did you start out in a line of sex work you thought you would want to continue in, or were you treading water and learning with a plan to change it up? Club jumping counts here. Can you talk about why?
I guess so. I club-jumped out of necessity, and now I work in nonclinical health care as my main gig. I want to impact the industry in a way that truly offers collective healing for a population of marginalized people as well as an autonomous zone for creating revenue.

What are some songs that were popular or that you loved when you first started doing sex work?
Oh my God, "What a Time to be Alive" had just come out, and Future and Drake have a lot to do with how I move my body.

How has sex work—the way you do it, the way you think it's perceived and understood by outsiders, and the community of sex workers you know (if any)—changed since you started?
I think between my specific generation of hoes and you, Matilda, it would actually be so fun to talk about. I grew up during the Internet,[1] so most of my whoring is Internet whoring. The club sucks when you're Black in the South. I will say when I started dancing it was like a high school reunion, and I think a lot of the club drama was just because we went from being mad at each other for stuff from tenth grade to stealing tips and club boyfriends. Too much too fast.

What music do you listen to to get pumped for work?
"City girls make em wish like ray j." ["Said Sum," by Moneybagg Yo featuring City Girls and DaBaby]

What do you do to relax after a bad shift or client?
I firmly believe in showering after dealing with people as a good rule of thumb, in sex work or otherwise.

Do you remember your first big money purchase with sex work money? What was it? How did you feel?
Never had one. My hustle money all comes together, and to this day I'm still a broke woman.

Do you feel like having done sex work has given you certain skills that are useful in your day-to-day or non-swing life that others don't have? What are some of them? Are there disadvantages from sex work that also come up? If there are, will you elaborate on them?

I'm gonna take it back to ancestry. Sex work is also in my lineage, and so I know if I want to, I can make sex drip off my aura and intoxicate the entire room. Consequently, I struggle with the line of performing and genuinely experiencing pleasure. I'm so good at faking a good time, I sometimes worry I don't know what a good time is.

What do you think would make sex workers' lives better or easier or safer (or all three)?

The same thing that would make anyone's lives safer, easier, or better: health care, housing, and human decency. People over profit. Defunding the police and refunding the community so that sex workers, who are just people, can live their lives.

Do you feel like you're a part of a larger community of sex workers? In person or on the Internet?

Absolutely, and it's an honor.

How do you see power dynamics play out in your community? What kind of workers are valued by other sex workers around you, and what kind of work is most valued?

If I am being completely honest about the whorearchy in the South, it's the white women who fuck for free and post for three dollars who seem the loudest on the Internet, and in real life. So loud, who can figure out where the rest of us go? If you're a white swer reading this, I wish to you a merry "be quiet sometimes." Abolish the whorearchy unless we putting BIPOC trans people first.

If you work in a place with a manager, what are they like? What are their interactions with the sex workers they "manage" like?

I'm gonna say this as a sex worker who has worked in many industries. In regular jobs, I fucked and flirted with multiple people in "management." In clubs, the managers get to fuck us over and flirt with ruining our lives.

Do you feel involved in sex worker activism or organizing? Do you want to be?

Not yet, but I'm working on it. I believe I can tie it into my work legitimately, and it's my deepest desire to do so, so that I can feel like I am living authentically. I'm a sexy spirit, I love to learn, and I'm passionate about both reproductive and healing justice. I hope to live to a time where I feel comfortable talking about the industry.

What kind of organizing goals are prioritized by the sex workers around you?
Organizing against one another, and that's: "What Is Class Consciousness, Alex?"

Regardless of whether you're involved in activism or organizing, what do you see as important goals for us to work toward?
Empowering sex workers to get into office, creating community space for us, women-owned sex shops, women-owned clubs.

What do you think are barriers to achieving those goals?
The barriers that prohibit women and trans people from achieving the exact same goals, with the added sticky note of "unlovable whore" on top.

How are you coping with our current reality?
It was always awful, wasn't it? If not for my son, I don't know what I would have done.

What would you like to see from white sex workers moving forward? Individually and/or as a community and/or as organizers?
Oh my God, I want them to use their platforms to amplify, listen, and otherwise be quiet! I have such a knee-jerk reaction to white sex workers using sex work as an oppression token, and I am willing to admit that's up to me to iron out in therapy, but it's truly toxic to the industry. Sex workers don't need help with our image, and now that the Internet is what it is and screaming into the void is more accessible than ever, it seems like they are the only ones screaming some days.

Note
1   Editor's Note: I know what you mean, but I also love that you think of me as pre-Internet. This conversation would be fun! Next book.

Waiting to Be Rescued from My Office Job

Emily Dall'Ora Warfield

I hate my job. I spend my days waiting for them to end. The emotional toll the work is taking on me is starting to degrade my spirit.

I'm a legal secretary.

Prior to this and several excruciatingly long months of unemployment, I was a sex worker. I quit because I was moving in with my boyfriend and we were both worried about what would happen to his custody of his child if I were ever arrested.

The relationship didn't last; my retirement did. I hadn't liked being a sex worker either, and I was eager to move on. I thought I had found something better. I had just found something different.

The biggest difference between sex work and office work, and the biggest benefit to the latter, is that I no longer worry about my physical safety. In this job, I have never been trafficked, illegally fined, forced to pay to take a sick day, verbally harassed, sexually assaulted, threatened, blackmailed, or nearly arrested, as I have been in the sex industry because of criminalization. I don't have to screen the lawyers I work with to try to weed out the ones who would assault me. I also obviously no longer worry about arrest, and I've started to wonder why: why is no one trying to "rescue" me from my job through handcuffs if I find it even more demoralizing than sex work?

Afterparty, by Ellis Burnheart

The main thing that gets to me—something that was never a problem with sex work—is the grinding boredom. I sit at a computer all day editing dry legal documents. The most exciting thing that ever happens is running out of paper clips, because then I get to go to the supply closet on the second floor. Truly the best thing I can say about my days is that they're eventually over.

At first, I thought this routine was tolerable. At least, it was preferable to the poverty and ceaseless anxiety of unemployment. I made it through the first few months just being grateful to have a job. Then the obvious set in: the days were going to keep on going, one Word document after another, for eight hours, eight hours, eight hours, endlessly. Once this settled under my skin, sometime around last February, something in me started to change.

I've recently charted that change. At my therapist's urging, I read through parts of my Twitter archive, trying to track my progress over the past year and a half since my breakup with my ex. I had thought it would be the time around the breakup that would be hardest to read, but it was the tweets from last February onward that hurt to revisit. Throughout the breakup and the aftermath, throughout the unemployment, through large life changes and daily struggles, I was depressed, but I still sounded like myself. I talked about the same subjects with the same passion. Several months after I started working, my tweets dropped off, not because I was at work (I certainly wasted enough time at my desk staring at my phone), but because I had nothing to say. My mind had started to empty. The hours spent staring at a screen were changing my thought patterns, depleting my passions, numbing my emotions. Sex work was often emotionally draining, and the violence of criminalization was occasionally traumatizing, but it never left me feeling like a different person.

The biggest benefit to sex work—one I appreciated while I was doing it although perhaps couldn't fully appreciate until now—was time. No matter how I felt about sex work or the ugly circumstances surrounding it, I never spent enough time doing it for it to take over my mind. No matter how emotionally draining I found it or how anxiety-inducing it was to screen out violent offenders and cops, all of that was over in no more than twelve to fifteen hours per week. Even when I was working shifts at a house dungeon, I spent most of my time reading, writing, and dicking around online. I had the time to be myself, to not get lost in my work.

The civilian nine-to-five doesn't offer such luxury. Now it takes me two days to earn what I used to make in an hour, two full days of sitting at my desk formatting Word documents. I am reprimanded if I insert extra spaces, or if I mishear a word in a lawyer's dictation, or if the margins of a table are a little too big or a little too small. I try to focus on details but can only focus for so long before I turn in an inevitably imperfect piece of work and then sit at my desk with nothing to do. (I was told that reading a book looks unprofessional.) I pace myself through the endless hours with treats like a cup of French vanilla coffee from the Keurig or a bag of Doritos chips from the vending machine. Some of the days of doing nothing much are so draining for me with my depression that I go to bed as soon as I get home. Then I wake up and do it all again.

I hardly have time for a social life or a hobby, for any connection or creativity. Throughout the few moments I still own—mostly on the weekends—time moves differently. I am hyperaware of every precious second passing, and they always speed by. I try to take full advantage, but mostly what that looks like is drinking too much. A few months ago, I woke up with a hangover after a night out with a friend for the first time in years, because I had tried to fit an entire week of life into a couple of hours.

And for the first time, I've done something for money that left me feeling truly disgusted with myself: I edited several legal briefs petitioning for a new pipeline that local environmental groups are strongly opposing. I've never done something so against my own moral code before, and I'm so ashamed that I haven't mentioned it to anyone until now. I admit to it not because I think I deserve forgiveness—I made my choice, constrained as it was—but only because I think the world should know it needs a new word for "an immoral woman; a venal or unscrupulous person."

But I'm not a hapless victim of the legal industry. I enrolled in grad school this fall to get a degree that will hopefully land me a job I mostly enjoy that comports with my ethical values. I've more than toyed with the idea of quitting this job and returning to sex work. Last February, I paid for a professional photo shoot. Then SESTA passed, and I wavered. But grad school has made the choice for me: starting next fall, I'll have to do unpaid field work twenty hours per week, which means I'll be unable to hold a full-time job. I plan on starting sex work again in three months, at the beginning of the spring semester. It feels like a light at the end of the tunnel.

With this hope of working a job I dislike for only a few hours per week on the horizon, I've started to come back into myself again. I've been writing more, thinking more. Now what I mostly think about is: Why is being a legal secretary, something so depleting, so soul-crushing, also perfectly legal? Why does no one judge me for my choice to continue working this job or fret about how it might be impacting me? We've moralized sexuality in such a way that monetizing it is considered uniquely hurtful when the truth is that most jobs under capitalism are violent in some way. Needing to work to survive is a kind of coercion anathema to consent. It's not a problem we can criminalize our way out of. We can only work toward a better society, one in which the shitty jobs abolish themselves because no one needs to work them anymore.

Until then, if you need me, I'll be at my desk.

Janis's Response

So much of this piece resonated with me. I worked civilian jobs all through college, but instead of the legal world, I worked in health-care administration. In undergrad, this looked like reception work in two different eye doctors' offices, one on the Upper East Side, where our patients were mostly well off, privileged white folks, some of whom were incredibly rude to the admin staff. At nineteen years old, I had to learn how to smile in the face of someone—a judge, wearing a floor-length fur coat—who angrily told me I was incompetent for not forging my employer's signature on her daughter's eye exam so that she could renew her license (the doctor was out of the country on holiday). Phrases like "Kill them with kindness" or "You catch more bees with honey than vinegar" don't come naturally to me; I'm more inclined to dish right back whatever is dealt to me, regardless of the perceived difference in status between me and whoever the hell they think they are. I worked in health-care administration for close to ten years before I started stripping, and every time I had to do this, had to try to assert my boundaries and my right to be treated with respect without endangering my job, my livelihood, my ability to survive, it felt like swallowing poison. Like Emily, I was also drinking a lot, after work and on the weekends, to deal with the emotional toll of my nine-to-five job.

It wasn't until I started stripping that my life started moving in the direction I wanted it to. I started stripping to supplement my freelance writing income (which was minuscule) and my work as a youth counselor at a homeless shelter for queer and trans youth (which barely paid minimum wage). Like Emily, I also experienced violence, misogyny, and risk at the club: being groped by clients, being verbally harassed and manipulated by the club owner and security staff, wondering what the heck would happen if my club were ever raided by police. And yet, when a customer was disrespectful, I could talk back. At times, I even physically defended myself. Part of my training as a health-care admin was "QTIP": quit taking it personally. At the club, on a bad night or after a particularly bad interaction with a customer, my coworkers would hug me, play with my hair, dab away my tears, and help me fix up my makeup. The refrain was never "Quit taking it personally." There was space for my rage, commiseration because we'd all experienced it, and a reminder of why we were there: to stack our paper and get gone.

All the vitriol I had to swallow as a health-care admin, had to push down and suppress, was given space and witnessed, rather than invalidated, at the club. Sex work helped pay for my sex education certificate and helped me pay for grad school, where I too was working twenty unpaid hours a week over the course of two years. Sex work helped me pay for my basic needs—food, rent—and pay off my loans. It was the way I built a life for myself free of patients, customers, and bosses—a life from which I no longer feel like I need to escape.

The High Cost of Cheap Labor

Melissa Ditmore

Sex work is an income-generating activity; it can be a business with a lot of overhead and structure, including support staff with official identification and taxes; it can be as simple as a person standing on the sidewalk. Most sex work falls on a spectrum between these two extremes. People overwhelmingly turn to sex work to generate income, often because they have difficulty with the structure of some workplaces or because they are not earning a living wage at a "straight" job. I coauthored a number of reports for the Sex Workers Project, and we found that for many, the sex industry supplements earnings from low-paying jobs.

When Juhu Thukral and I wrote *Revolving Door* and *Behind Closed Doors*, we found that only one-third of the people interviewed reported earning enough money to live from their other jobs before engaging in sex work. In *Revolving Door: An Analysis of Street-Based Prostitution in New York City*, we wrote:

> Occupations held by interviewees were usually low-paid, entry-level positions that did not provide enough money to live. The majority of subjects had held more than one job in the past.... The most common job previously held by respondents was waitressing. Examples of other food service-related jobs that subjects had held,

Repeal, by Anonymous

but which did not pay them a living wage, included working in fast-food restaurants; managing a restaurant that was part of a large fast-food chain; and bartending.

Many of the low-paying jobs cited would not be deemed skilled-labor, including working in a hotel; retail sales in department and clothing stores; odd jobs; security; secretarial and receptionist positions; nurse's aide; school aide; and babysitting. Licensed or skilled labor that respondents reported did not provide them sufficient income for their needs included hairdressing and makeup; work in entertainment including singing, drag shows, and dancing; positions in real estate; working as a dental assistant; and working as an emergency medical technician. Respondents additionally reported having worked in an amusement park and at a printing house.

Researchers were told that some people were able to live on these wages because they were living with family members and had few expenses, or that their wages were used to support other income, such as public assistance or alimony.[1]

In *Behind Closed Doors: An Analysis of Indoor Sex Work in New York City*, we added:

> These jobs ranged from low-wage labor to well-paid career tracks. The low-wage end of the spectrum included such jobs as babysitting, cleaning, passing out fliers, and food service. Freelance work included graphic design and writing, as well as the arts. Respondents in middle class careers included civil servants, construction and electrical workers. The most well paid worked in real estate and accounting.[2]

While these reports are over ten years old, more recent research found that impoverished people continue to trade sex in order to provide for themselves and their families.[3] Supplementing other money with sex work is universal; for example, the French have the term *étoiles filantes*, or "shooting stars," for women who use sex work to get by when they have run out of money at the end of the month. Transgender people face discrimination in securing any kind of job and are twice as likely to be unemployed as cisgender people.[4] These are reasons transgender people are overrepresented in the sex trades: sometimes they are supplementing other income, and sometimes sex work is their only income.

Many people in the sex trades face greater economic difficulty today because the legal environment has become more hostile with the closure of many websites used by sex workers to advertise and to vet potential clients. Sex workers advertise to reach clients. At its most basic, this can be standing on a "stroll," where people expect to find sex workers. Sex workers used low-cost advertising on Craigslist and BackPage and paid more for ads on specialized sites like RentBoy.com and myRedBook.[5] Various advertising sites have worked to address trafficking, including partnering with organizations advocating for missing children, but they have been asked to eliminate all sex work ads instead of just preventing posts advertising sex with minors and posts advertising other nonconsensual activities that meet the definition of sex trafficking. These sites were specifically targeted by anti-sex work campaigners who sought to close them using federal laws.[6] The campaigns culminated in the passage of a law that criminalizes the hosts of any site that may be used by sex workers to meet clients, even if that is not the main purpose of the site. This is how the passage of FOSTA/SESTA in 2018 led to the closure of a site for people who cosplay as anthropomorphized animals for fear that any hint of prostitution on their message board could render the site owner legally liable.[7] Before websites used by sex workers were targeted by federal law, the print ads that gave BackPage its name and their online successors were targeted by feminist organizations, including the New York City National Organization of Women,[8] but few alternative weekly publications could afford to cut the lucrative back-page ads for massage parlors and escorts. This campaign took the form of an "antiprostitution ad pledge" prepared by NOW NYC, without concern for the economic needs of the women who support themselves and their families through sexual commerce. Anti-sex work activists strategically target sex workers' livelihoods, and the people most hurt by these campaigns are those with the fewest options: people trading sex to survive, transgender people, people who are dependent on substances, undocumented people, and people with few skills or training for other gainful employment.

The global coronavirus pandemic of 2020 cost many jobs and compounded fiscal hardship. "Social distancing," keeping a few feet apart, has become part of everyday life during the COVID-19 pandemic and has limited some forms of sex work. Most sex workers have taken up the new "safe sex," but in-person, more physical forms of sex work are newly dangerous due to contagion. While online sex work may carry on, there is more competition now as people move into these platforms.[9] One person in the top 20 percent of earners on the OnlyFans platform explained that even though she is a high earner, her income from this platform would not cover most people's rent. She has not made $500 in a month, and she explained that the top 2 percent earn between $2,000 and $4,000 per month, while the top 0.01 percent receive tens of thousands of dollars per month.[10] Some of these high earners are celebrities like hip-hop artist and former stripper Cardi B and actor Michael Jordan.[11] With estimates ranging between 450,000 and over 1 million content providers using the platform,[12] that is between 4,500 and 10,000 people earning upwards of $100,000 in a year,[13] but as in other creative fields like music and acting, many strive while very few thrive.

Some people turn to sex work to supplement other wages, like the New York City emergency medical technician who also had an OnlyFans account.[14] The scandal is less that she performed online but that a highly skilled worker is so poorly paid that she needs a second job. In cases like this, sex work functions as supplemental income or a social safety net. Considering the fast-food employees who reported not earning enough to live from their jobs, including a manager at a national fast-food corporation, it's clear that that sex work also subsidizes corporations that do not pay their workers a living wage. However, with sex workers on popular platforms earning under $500 per month, it's unclear whether any job subsidizes another. Instead, it seems wages in the gig economy are lower in many more sectors than people without experience in either the gig economy or the sex trades imagine, with formerly well-paid working-class jobs in manufacturing disappearing or being devalued with lower earnings. Take, for example, the medic whose job could have been a full-time position with benefits before health care became a for-profit endeavor; jobs like these have transformed many careers in health care and other jobs that were once considered callings into gigs.

Sex work has long been a gig for many, with flexible hours, but twenty-first-century wages are so low that every person is required to hustle for multiple jobs to survive. This reflects an acceptance of "ordinary poverty"[15] as normal rather than address the reality of an impoverished underclass, as in the social movements of earlier eras. What started as an effort to end welfare in the 1990s, instead of combating poverty, has led to, in the twenty-first century, the transformation of formerly middle-class jobs with wages so depressed that full-time workers are eligible for federal benefits, transferring wealth to executives and shareholders instead of workers. The acceptance of this impoverishment of millions of workers has contributed to an influx of people trying to supplement low-wage jobs with side hustles, including sex work. Exploitation of labor is clear when workers are paid so little they are eligible for federal benefits, as with many fast-food companies in the United States, leading to the Fight for 15 Campaign to raise fast food workers' wages to fifteen dollars per hour.[16] This was supported by 60 percent of Florida voters in 2020.[17] When workers remain eligible for federal benefits and the public company that employs them pays its shareholders dividends,[18] this is corporate welfare in which the taxpayer pays twice: first for the federal benefits of the employees and second for the lesser taxes, as low as 15 percent on capital gains like stock market dividends, rather than the payroll taxes (approximately double) that a higher wage would offer, along with the increased spending by the people who earn that wage. The wages offered for fast-food jobs and other low-paying work leaves no room for debate about how the demand for cheap labor has skewed the American labor market so that workers may turn to sex work or federal benefits to supplement their meager wages, which have stagnated for nearly fifty years while executive compensation has risen disproportionately.[19]

The demand for cheap labor also extends to more extreme forms of exploitation, such as unpaid labor. The most extreme examples of workplace exploitation are defined under US law as "human trafficking." Trafficking refers to the use of force, fraud, or coercion,[20] including threats of violence as well as physical violence, to profit or otherwise benefit from the activities of another, in either the labor sector or the sex trades. Additionally, any commercial sex act committed by anyone under the age of eighteen in the United States is per se trafficking.

Trafficking is a form of extreme exploitation that happens to people of all ages and ethnic backgrounds from every part of the world. Trafficking is found in all forms of work, from computer programming to working in tomato fields and domestic work, as well as in the sex trades.[21] Undocumented people are especially vulnerable to trafficking, because threats of deportation in addition to job loss are used if someone complains about poor working conditions. Race and gender also figure;

unskilled and poorly paid work is frequently performed by people of color who earn less in the sex trades than their white counterparts.[22] Sexual harassment and assault are common problems for women working in agriculture.[23] In the United States, impoverished people are a nearly permanent underclass that comprises all races and identities.

Workers in any sector who do not know that worker rights are for everyone, including people with irregular status, are also vulnerable to exploitation. Those who are not part of collective movements like unions or guilds are particularly vulnerable, as we have shown in the gig economy. Workers may be vulnerable to sexual harassment and abuse, especially those who are geographically or socially isolated, like live-in domestic workers, agricultural workers in remote fields, and people who are considered sexually exploitable or discreditable because of stigma, like sex workers and people forced to sell sex. Domestic workers are particularly vulnerable to sexual harassment and abuse because they work in private places like homes and in private situations, but they are not who people think of when we imagine victims of trafficking, even when their circumstances meet the definition of trafficking. This cultural blind spot prevents our conceiving of the full range of victims. Vulnerability in the workplace can include vulnerability to sexual harassment and abuse, and those targeted with such abuse are typically at greater risk than those around them, either because of age and inexperience or a lack of skills or lack of understanding of their rights, or they may be trapped in a situation they cannot leave, for reasons related to language barriers, being unaware of their geographic surroundings, such as the neighborhood. In these latter instances, people in abusive situations are vulnerable to their employers, especially if they live with their employers.

Contemporary trafficking is related to historical forms of cheap labor, including indentured servitude and chattel slavery.[24] However, the word *trafficking* evokes the idea of young girls forced to sell sex, which garners more attention than other labor abuses that fit the definition of trafficking. Neglecting abuse in the workplace enables exploitation and trafficking to carry on unchecked. While the popular idea of trafficking focuses on protecting children, the 445 remaining children separated from their parents at the US border between 2017 and 2019 and held in squalid conditions demonstrates that care for children is not the motivation behind the attachment to the antitrafficking rescue narra-tive.[25] Our societal focus on sex comes at the expense of abused workers and immigrant children in US custody. In fact, the US violated its own antitrafficking law by deporting some of the thousands of children to countries that were not their own.[26] The focus on protecting children is proven a sham in the case of children separated from their families at the border; these children were not helped, even as their situations demanded rescue from detention.

The focus on sex trafficking overshadows labor trafficking even though sexual abuse and assault is common in labor trafficking, some-times meeting the definition of sex trafficking. Cheap labor is actually quite expensive, because the combination of labor exploitation, corporate tax avoidance, the eligibility of corporate employees for federal benefits, and workplace abuses including sexual harassment and assault represent additional costs not calculated when discussing low-wage work. The US government has multiple tools to change this situation without changing law or policy. Any administration could ameliorate working conditions by emphasizing the enforcement of labor laws for all workers, including addressing labor trafficking. Laws addressing sexual assault could be enforced without causing victims, including people without legal status, to fear reporting, and could promote coming forward to report violent crimes. Adjusting the federal minimum wage would require Congress to act so that fewer full-time employees would be impoverished; however, twenty-nine state governments and Washington, DC, have increased their minimum wages without losing minimum-wage jobs or forcing the closure of workplaces, and voter referendums have demonstrated wide support for such measures. Political will to make these advances may be lacking, but grassroots movements are working for these changes and more, including multiple state-level efforts across the country to improve conditions for sex workers by decriminalizing sex work. Cheap labor is very expensive indeed, and while slavery and exploitation are part of our history, we can eliminate worker exploitation from our future.

Notes

1   Juhu Thukral and Melissa Ditmore, *Revolving Door: An Analysis of Street-Based Prostitution in New York City* (New York: Urban Justice Center, 2005), 55, https://sexworkersproject.org/publications/reports/revolving-door.

2   Juhu Thukral and Melissa Ditmore, *Behind Closed Doors: An Analysis of Indoor Sex Work in New York City* (New York: Urban Justice Center, 2005), 34, https://sexworkersproject.org/publications/reports/behind-closed-doors.

3   Kari R. Olson, Jessica E. Justman, Yunmi Chung, Kimberly A. Parker, Carol E. Golin, and Stephanie Lykes, "The Logic of Exchange Sex among Women Living in Poverty," chap. 9 in *Poverty in the United States*, ed. Ann O'Leary and Paula M. Frew (New York: Springer, 2017), https://doi.org/10.1007/978-3-319-43833-7_9.

4   Movement Advancement Project, National Center for Transgender Equality, Human Rights Campaign, and Center for American Progress, *A Broken Bargain for Transgender Workers*, September 2013, https://www.lgbtmap.org/transgender-workers.

5   Merrit Kennedy, "Craigslist Shuts Down Personals Section after Congress Passes Bill on Trafficking," *The Two-Way*, National Public Radio, March 23, 2018, https://www.npr.org/sections/thetwo-way/2018/03/23/596460672/craigslist-shuts-down-personals-section-after-congress-passes-bill-on-traffickin; Christine Biederman, "Inside BackPage.com's Vicious Battle with the Feds," *Wired*, June 18, 2019, https://www.wired.com/story/inside-backpage-vicious-battle-feds; Anonymous, "Rentboy Wasn't My 'Brothel.' It Was a Tool to Stay Alive in This Economy of Violence," *Guardian*, September 1, 2015, https://www.theguardian.com/commentisfree/2015/sep/01/rentboy-online-brothel-tool-economy-sex-work.

6   Christine Biederman, "Inside BackPage.com's Vicious Battle with the Feds."

7   Pounced.org was a dating site for "furries," people who cosplay as anthropomorphized animals. After the passage of FOSTA/SESTA, the site voluntarily shut down. Samantha Cole, "Furry Dating Site Shuts Down Because of FOSTA," *Motherboard* (tech blog), *Vice*, April 2, 2018, https://www.vice.com/en/article/8xk8m4/furry-dating-site-pounced-is-down-fosta-sesta.

8   Lenore Skenazy, "Fumigating New York's Weeklies," *New York Sun*, August 15, 2007, https://www.nysun.com/new-york/fumigating-new-yorks-weeklies/60598.

9   Gillian Friedman, "Jobless, Selling Nudes Online, and Still Struggling," *New York Times*, January 13, 2021, https://www.nytimes.com/2021/01/13/business/onlyfans-pandemic-users.html.

10   Personal correspondence, January 1 and 3, 2021.

11   Canela Lopez and Kat Tenbarge, "Michael B. Jordan and 15 Other Celebrities Who Have Made OnlyFans Pages," *Insider*, November 26, 2020, https://www.insider.com/blac-chyna-and-celebrities-who-have-made-onlyfans-profiles-2020-5#model-blac-chyna-charges-fans-50-a-month to access-her-onlyfans-page-which-already-has-a-few-foot-fetish-videos-on-it-1.

12   "OnlyFans Statistics—Users, Revenue and Usage Stats," Influencer Marketing Hub, December 14, 2020, https://influencermarketinghub.com/onlyfans-stats; Lucas Shaw, "OnlyFans Is a Billion-Dollar Media Giant Hiding in Plain Sight," *Bloomberg*, December 5, 2020, https://www.bloomberg.com/news/articles/2020-12-05/celebrities-like-cardi-b-could-turn-onlyfans-into-a-billion-dollar-media-company?sref=3Ac2yX40.

13   Consider Monica Huldt, who describes her use of the site as nonstop work. Mia Jankowicz, "We Spoke to a Woman Earning More Than $100,000 a Year Selling Explicit Content on OnlyFans—This Is Exactly How She Makes Her Money,"

Business Insider, March 14, 2020, https://www.businessinsider.com/onlyfans-monica-huldt-describes-how-makes-money-2020-3.

14 Lucy Diavolo, "AOC Said 'Sex Work Is Work' in Response to *NY Post* Hit Piece on Paramedic with an Onlyfans," *Teen Vogue*, December 16, 2020, https://www.teenvogue.com/story/aoc-sex-work-is-work-new-york-post-hit-piece-paramedic-onlyfans; Alexandra Ocasio Cortez, "Leave her alone. The actual scandalous headline here is 'Medics in the United States need two jobs to survive,'" Twitter, December 13, 2021, https://twitter.com/aoc/status/1338336656953368579; Dean Balsamini with Susan Edelman, "NYC Medic Helped Make Ends Meet with Racy Onlyfans Side Gig," *New York Post*, December 12, 2020, https://nypost.com/2020/12/12/nyc-medic-helped-make-ends-meet-with-racy-onlyfans-side-gig.

15 William DiFazio described "ordinary poverty" as the normalization of poverty, demonstrated by the overall acceptance of increasingly hopeless situations for the poor, in his book *Ordinary Poverty: A Little Food and Cold Storage* (Philadelphia: Temple University Press, 2005).

16 See https://fightfor15.org.

17 Lorie Konish, "Florida Passes $15 per Hour Minimum Wage," *CNBC*, November 6, 2020, https://www.cnbc.com/2020/11/06/florida-passes-15-per-hour-minimum-wage-economists-seek-national-trend.html.

18 Tonya Garcia, "McDonald's Shares Jump after Earnings Beat Expectations and Dividend Raised," *MarketWatch*, November 9, 2020, https://www.marketwatch.com/story/mcdonalds-shares-jump-after-earnings-beat-expectations-and-dividend-raised-2020-11-09.

19 David Hope and Julian Limberg, *The Economic Consequences of Major Tax Cuts for the Rich*, International Inequalities Institute Working Papers (London: London School of Economics and Political Science, 2020), 55, http://eprints.lse.ac.uk/107919/; Drew DeSilver, "For Most U.S. Workers, Real Wages Have Barely Budged in Decades," *Pew Research Center Fact Tank*, August 7, 2018, https://www.pewresearch.org/fact-tank/2018/08/07/for-most-us-workers-real-wages-have-barely-budged-for-decades.

20 From the Trafficking Victims Protection Act of 2000.

21 Ethan Baron, "H-1B Worker in San Jose Forced to Pay Own Salary, Threatened with Deportation: Lawsuit," *Mercury News*, December 19, 2018, https://www.mercurynews.com/2018/12/19/h-1b-worker-in-san-jose-forced-to-pay-own-salary-threatened-with-deportation-lawsuit; "Anti-Slavery Program," Coalition of Immokalee Workers, accessed November 10, 2020, http://ciw-online.org/slavery; Ariel Ramchandani, "Diplomats Are Getting Away with Abusing Their Children's Nannies," *Atlantic*, May 21, 2018, https://www.theatlantic.com/business/archive/2018/05/diplomats-abuse-domestic-workers/559739.

22 Siobhan Brooks, *Unequal Desires: Race and Erotic Capital in the Stripping Industry* (Albany, NY: SUNY Press, 2010); Mireille Miller-Young, *A Taste for Brown Sugar: Black Women in Pornography* (Durham, NC: Duke University Press, 2014).

23 Ariel Ramchandani, "There's a Sexual Harassment Epidemic on America's Farms," *Atlantic*, January 29, 2018, https://www.theatlantic.com/business/archive/2018/01/agriculture-sexual-harassment/550109.

24 Melissa Ditmore, "Today's Efforts to Combat Human Trafficking Reflect Historical Racism and Sexism," *Rewire News Group*, January 11, 2011, https://rewirenewsgroup. com/article/2011/01/11/todays-efforts-combat-human-trafficking-reflect-historical-racism-sexism.

25 The Republican administration separated thousands of immigrant children from their parents between 2017 and 2019. At the time of writing in November 2020, many of these children had been deported. Caitlyn Dickerson, "Hundreds of Immigrant Children Have Been Taken from Parents at U.S. Border," *New York Times*, April 20, 2018, https://www.nytimes.com/2018/04/20/us/immigrant-children-separation-ice.html; Caitlyn Dickerson, "Parents of 545 Children Separated at the Border Cannot Be Found," *New York Times*, October 21, 2020, https://www.nytimes.com/2020/10/21/us/migrant-children-separated.html? action=click&module=RelatedLinks&pgtype=Article; Michael D. Shear, Abby Goodnough, and Maggie Haberman, "Trump Retreats on Separating Families, but Thousands May Remain Apart," *New York Times*, June 20, 2018, https://www. nytimes.com/2018/06/20/us/politics/trump-immigration-children-executive-order.html; Aishvarya Kavi, "Parents of 445 Children Separated by Trump Still Not Found, Filing Says," *New York Times*, April 7, 2021, https://www.nytimes. com/2021/04/07/us/migrant-children-separated-border.html; Caitlyn Dickerson, "'There Is a Stench': Soiled Clothes and No Baths for Migrant Children at a Texas Center," *New York Times*, June 21, 2019, https://www.nytimes.com/2019/06/21/ us/migrant-children-border-soap.html.

26 Caitlyn Dickerson, "10 Years Old, Tearful and Confused after a Sudden Deportation," *New York Times*, May 20, 2020, updated October 21, 2020, https://www.nytimes.com/2020/05/20/us/coronavirus-migrant-children-unaccompanied-minors.html?action=click&module=RelatedLinks&pgtype= Article; Caitlyn Dickerson, "U.S. Expels Migrant Children from Other Countries to Mexico," *New York Times*, October 30, 2020, updated November 3, 2020, https:// www.nytimes.com/2020/10/30/us/migrant-children-expulsions-mexico.html?.

Protect, Believe, Support, by Jelena Vermilion

Jelena Vermilion

Do you remember the first time you learned that selling sex or performing sexy was a way to make money?
Yes!

How did you find out, and what was your immediate reaction?
I think I became vaguely aware growing up, when I watched *Milk Money* (1994) too many times—on VHS—as a kid, I was pretty relaxed about it, but more importantly, I was fascinated by the power and gender dynamics. This knowledge was solidified when I became exposed to *The Secret Diary of a Call Girl* (2007-2011) in my late teens.

Did you know it would be something that you would do for income at that point?
Not in the slightest. I was fascinated, but at that time I didn't foresee myself entering the industry.

When did you decide to trade sex/ualized services?
I became homeless for three months in 2014 after experiencing incarceration, so I started sex work in order to get myself an apartment, some stability, etc. I now continue to do sex work for a variety of reasons,

including but not limited to: flexible working hours, better wages, and because I've experienced discrimination in other employment, and education.

Did you first start working in a space or field where there were other sex workers around, or did you work in isolation? What was that like?
My very first experiences were with another woman who was already doing sex work. I met her at the homeless shelter I was staying at, and she and I eventually stayed in a hotel room together. I was just learning how to start advertising, and then we were both working. After a period of time, she became exploitative and was expecting me to pay her a cut of each client's payment to me, so I eventually started working independently, out of hotels at first.

Did you start out in a line of sex work you thought you would want to continue in, or were you treading water and learning with a plan to change it up? Club jumping counts here. Can you talk about why?
I started with full-service work and was scouted from my ad to perform in pornography. I found it helpful to take on as much porn work as was possible, until the culture changed and less work was available. I am satisfied with providing full-service because it actually feels like an equitable exchange to me, most times. It feels like honest work to me.

What are some songs that were popular or that you loved when you first started doing sex work?
I really loved Donna Summer's "Bad Girls." I have the vinyl record now. The album art, the lyrics, and the esoteric meanings really entertain and please me.

How has sex work—the way you do it, the way you think it's perceived and understood by outsiders, and the community of sex workers you know (if any)—changed since you started?
- I spend a lot more time enforcing boundaries and not allowing my time to be wasted by bad-faith actors looking for freebies. That's a big change that I've grown to implement.
- I do feel there has been a bit of a shift in the consciousness surrounding sex work for the last decade specifically. I feel there are more

accepting views toward it, but confusion about the specifics of potential reform.

- Many of us have died, incurred state violence, and experienced trauma. Many of us have become homeless or incarcerated. We have had to hustle in many ways, while repression has raged on. I feel we are coming to a paradigm shift.

Do you feel like you're a part of a larger community of sex workers? In person or on the Internet?

I do feel affinity to/with other sex workers, and I do visualize this fragmented network of so-called *Lumpenproles*, both in person *and* on the Internet. It is affirming and validating to know—if frustrating—that the particular struggle(s) we experience is shared by other workers around the world.

How do you see power dynamics play out in your community? What kind of workers are valued by other sex workers around you, and what kind of work is most valued?

- Often bureaucracy in the name of the collective interest can get in the way of actual progress and material change. Many people are silenced, while those who posture for clout are glorified.
- Definitely those with class privilege: thin, white, able-bodied people who command high rates from clients.
- Care work, sexual and emotional labor. Anything to stroke the client—be it their ego or their loins.

Do you feel involved in sex worker activism or organizing? Do you want to be?

Yes, I am certainly involved in sex worker organizing. It can be exhausting and isolating. For me, it is not a question of if I *want* to be involved, but rather it feels necessary and like a solemn duty to work toward. Solidarity!

What kind of organizing goals are prioritized by the sex workers around you?

Securing material safety for ourselves, maintaining and defending our housing, status for migrant workers.

Regardless of whether you're involved in activism or organizing, what do you see as important goals for us to work toward?
Decriminalization as a first and vital step, and working toward improving the material working conditions for sex workers. Removing the immigration legislation that makes im/migrant workers liable to deportation for doing sex work, in Canada, and prioritizing the most marginalized sex workers, including Black, Indigenous, Asian, and otherwise racialized sex workers, im/migrant or undocumented sex workers, trans and nonbinary and two-spirit sex workers, disabled sex workers, fat sex workers, and sex workers who use drugs.

What do you think are barriers to achieving those goals?
The bureaucratic system and the "democracy" are huge barriers to reforming laws, as criminalization is a direct barrier for sex workers accessing health, legal, and social resources.

How are you coping with our current reality?
I try to dissociate when necessary. I also smoke a lot of cannabis. It is important for us to realize that the world is a fucked-up place and that it is understandable that we're heavily traumatized in varying ways.

What would you like to see from white sex workers moving forward? Individually and/or as a community and/or as organizers?
I'd like to see more white sex workers and organizers use their whiteness as a tool. If we are speaking to the media, have our messaging together and make sure we are representing underserved populations in the sex industry.

Do you feel like having done sex work has given you certain skills that are useful in your day-to-day or non-swing life that others don't have? What are some of them? Are there disadvantages from sex work that also come up? If there are, will you elaborate on them?
Skills sex workers collectively have:
- De-escalation
- Cyber security
- Self-defense knowledge
- Access to liberal pity
- Mitigating surveillance

- Harm reduction
- Care work
- Being critical
- Decisiveness
- Negotiation
- Manufacturing
- Cultivating intimacy
- Social engineering
- Graphic design
- Makeup artists
- Web designers
- Honed intuition
- SEO
- Dancing
- Identifying undercover cops
- Massage
- Being a muse
- Making escape plans
- Shoplifting
- Ability to be unassuming
- Disguise
- Navigating different geography
- Access to clandestine economies
- Herbalism
- Wordsmiths
- Deep research
- Code-switching
- Entertaining
- Healers and therapists
- Marketing specialists
- Sensing red flags
- Investigative skills and social parsing
- Financial wisdom
- Sexual health knowledge
- Mentorship
- Theater, film, and photography
- Spatial sense
- Hotel wisdom

- Hypervigilance
- Trespassing
- Teaching yourself new skills (autodidacts)
- Dissociation
- Effecting planning and packing
- Storytelling
- Record-keeping
- Flexible scheduling
- Stamina

Disadvantages: Burnout, stigma, judgment (nobody likes the naked truth à la Jean-Léon Gérôme's "Truth Coming Out of Her Well"). Catering to clients can take a lot of emotional and physical labor, so making sure to maintain strong boundaries and self-care in a meaningful and material way is paramount to health and longevity in this industry.

Cyntoia Brown and My Black Body

Naomi

I spent my teen years selling sex on the Internet. I grew up on the Craigslist erotic services section, finding men who would pay me for something I didn't take seriously, because I'd been robbed of the chance to do so. I'd been raped at twelve by my next-door neighbor after months of molestation and was subsequently passed around the neighborhood to two other perverts. One was an Albanian fella who definitely sold women, and he could have ended up trafficking me as well. In hindsight, my luck has been insane.

Cyntoia Brown's and Chrystul Kizer's stories feel too close to home to dismiss the connections. Brown killed one of her abusers at the age of sixteen; so did Kizer. When I was sixteen, I met a man on Yahoo! Personals who seemed nice enough. After a four-hour session, he didn't want to pay. He kicked me out of the house and I had to find my way home. He could have killed me, and I thought he would, because he grabbed me so hard to throw me out. That session could have been my last, and no one would have been the wiser. If I'd been abducted, my mom would have been looking for a ghost; she had no idea what I was doing.

Because of the demographics I fit into—Black, girl, and too young to be working in the first place—I was wary of telling anyone what I was doing. And even when I felt like I was in danger, I couldn't call the police without worrying about my Black body being meat for the carceral system to chew up and spit out. Calling the police because a session went wrong would have ruined my life. There is no class mobility for a poor Black woman with a prostitution charge on her record. Understanding this, it doesn't surprise me that both Chrystul and Cyntoia chose to leave the scene instead of calling police for assistance. Coerced or not, one of the first things you learn as a full-service sex worker is that cops are more dangerous than clients.

Knowing full well—or as well as an eighteen-year-old can—the possible consequences involved, and just trying to make my way out of poverty, I did dangerous shit constantly. Meeting someone at a Sonic or getting into an Uber they paid for (because you do not have the seventeen dollars it will cost, or do not have a smartphone, or do not have a debit card to set up an account) doesn't seem odd when you take into account how poverty erodes your access to even the most basic necessities. Poverty seems to be a recurring theme in these stories of sex work, survival sex work, and trafficking. The Mayflower Madam said, "A call girl is simply a woman who hates poverty more than she hates sin." But this speaks of an agency that a lot of us don't have, and it's important to acknowledge.

So many Black and brown girls are just trying to make it to tomorrow with as little pain as possible. Because of how our bodies are forced to navigate late capitalism, we find ourselves gambling with the very lives we are fighting to keep. Yes, my boyfriend sells me, but he feeds me. Yes, he beats me, but I'm not homeless.

In 2006, Cyntoia Brown was convicted of first-degree murder for shooting and killing Johnny Michael Allen, a forty-three-year-old man who'd hired her for sex. Brown says she believes Allen was reaching for his gun when she shot him. According to an amended petition for a writ of habeas corpus filed by Brown's legal team in 2015, twenty-four-year-old Garion "Cut Throat" McGlothen forced the young teenage Brown into transactional sex with other men and subjected her to physical and sexual abuse.

Brown was in jail for over a decade, and we are the same age.

Chrystul Kizer met Randall Volar, a thirty-four-year-old man, when she was sixteen. On the night of the killing, Chrystul traveled to his home in an Uber that he paid for, and she spent several hours there before shooting him in self-defense. Here as everywhere, we are the same woman.

The pseudo-positivist leanings of the judicial system are ill-suited to address the lived experiences of Black and brown folks, period. Add sex into that, and mix it up with poverty? A mess. I'm learning more and more how rare my story of having never been arrested is. The school-to-prison pipeline was built for girls just like me, and even outside of school, Black girls' bodies are rendered adult and profane before we get to decide for ourselves. So many of us are trying to shake free of state surveillance, and the state conjures new ways to remind us that we are seen and invisible constantly. This is a web designed to keep us bound, much like shackles.

Cyntoia was originally facing fifty-one years for defending her humanity but was released after fifteen in 2019. Chrystul fared a bit better, awaiting trial for two years before being released on a $400,000 bond that was paid by a Chicago-based bail fund in 2020. They served that time because the state sees us as nonhuman problems to be disappeared, not cared for.

Abolish the carceral system. Period. Our bodies deserve more than this.

Flamenca, by Manon

Manon

Do you remember the first time you learned that selling sex or performing sexy was a way to make money?

I was probably three or four years old. I remember my aunts telling me half-jokingly that I could grow up to be a famous flamenco dancer like Tia Tania if I would stop being so shy and get in the middle of the circle with my cousin and try out the hip and torso isolations that they would drunkenly and dramatically demonstrate at every family gathering. Flamenco (and other forms of dancing that flamenco is informed by) has been and continues to be considered one of the primary avenues for an otherwise extremely marginalized and disenfranchised group of people (Romani) to gain immediate monetary success.

Did you know it would be something that you would do for income at that point?

I always knew it was something that could be a sort of last-resort type of job, not because it was portrayed as particularly taboo in my family, but because first-generation immigrant children are expected to do better than their parents within the margins of the respectability politics demanded by capitalism, and only one of my parents had a high school diploma, so there was great expectation and hope that I would get into either a free or good college.

My grandmother and great-grandmother were full-service sex workers who worked outdoors and indoors as the area demanded, all over Europe and Africa in the early to mid-twentieth century. It was not fun for them, I gathered from family stories. I was always warned that it was very dangerous to become a sex worker. My dad told me and my sister—within the context of making a point about fascism and not sex work specifically—that as a kid living in Triana, the Gypsy neighborhood of Sevilla, he would hide when Franco's fascist police would ride through the Gypsy/red-light neighborhoods, "dragging prostitutes down the street by their hair." So there was a lot of well-intended Captain Save-a-Hooker sentiment expressed by my father throughout my childhood. My mom's side of the family are all radical hippies who have thought sex work should be decriminalized since at least before their arrival in the Americas. I remember overhearing the opinions of my maternal grandmother, who was a lesbian activist and nurse who worked in Oakland, Berkeley, and San Francisco. I remember her talking about treating women in the ER who were mainly Black, trans, and/or migrant sex workers and about how hateful the other medical professionals were toward them. I would say that I considered sex work of some form to be a viable potential option for me, either as a fast-cash side gig or in some kind of elevated, elegant, professional way, like being a dominatrix, I imagined, before I knew much about or was a sex worker.

When did you decide to trade sex/ualized services?

After having gotten myself into a nice school on not enough of a scholarship to avoid massive loans, I suffered a legitimate attempt on my life. Halfway through undergrad, I had a violent encounter with a wealthy Brentwood boy who thought I was stealing his girlfriend. He punched me in the face and threatened to kill me. This was the only time calling the cops saved me, and not because they showed up. I managed to somehow dial 911 visibly while being pinned to the passenger door of my car, and he backed off, running away. Unfortunately, his friends who witnessed it lied, and his father was a lawyer who threatened the administration into forcing me to either leave or continue taking classes with his son daily with no protections or schedule modifications, as that would have been an admission of guilt on his part. I wasn't protected under Title

IX because the incident hadn't occurred on campus. I very naively had been banking on an industrial design degree affording me entry into the upper echelons of the creative economy.

I moved back in with my dad in Northern California to help him sell our house. I became a preschool teacher. For six months, I drank DayQuil from the bottle and cleaned human shit off toys, plotting my next move, which led to the realization that I could transfer most of my current job skills to a more lucrative industry. I desperately wanted to avoid the cannabis trade, because my family would have been disappointed they'd had to become criminals only for me to repeat the cycle. I feel compelled to point out the irritating irony.

My best friend had started stripping and posted a selfie in a fox fur coat. I asked her if she thought I could do it, and she told me all I needed to know was how to be naked by the end of two songs and count cash in the dark. She told me that her stripper name was Bambi and to think of something that sounds similar to my real name in case I ever fuck up when meeting a customer. She bragged that a lot of high-profile Hollywood people frequented her club so the management liked to hire "classy" girls who were skinny and eloquent. So I drove back down to LA to become a stripper.

Did you first start working in a space or field where there were other sex workers around, or did you work in isolation? What was that like?
I entered sex work through Silver Reign Gentleman's Club. At the time, a glamorous Mexican girl named Yolanda who also did porn was living on Bambi's couch along with me. We were the same size, so she lent me a gold American Apparel bikini and a brand-new pair of black vinyl boots. Right before my audition, while Bambi was telling the DJ my songs, Yolanda pulled me by the hand into the customer bathroom, whipped out a bump on a glorious stiletto nail, and produced a liter of Camarena tequila from her Mary Poppins–like work bag.

"Take a shot and try to smile on stage without throwing up, and move like the air is honey. If the customers laugh at you, act as though you meant for them to." She slapped my ass up the dinky stairwell to the stage, where I floundered around to "Peaches," by the Stranglers. I was hired and made ten dollars off a topless dance. The manager came over to collect half, and he pointed to a beautiful redheaded woman sitting on a velvet couch with her rhinestone-encrusted pleasers slipped halfway off.

He told me she wanted to talk to me. I felt like I was in *The Godfather* for a minute, this woman commanded so much presence.

"My name is Scarlett." She outstretched a languid hand showing off perfect red nails. "I'm a Wiccan. You're, like, really pretty. Your friend watched my cats last weekend and told me about you. Do you wanna go to the Aveda Institute with me tomorrow to get free blowouts? Let's go smoke a bowl in my car, it's so dead in here right now."

I didn't see any Black women in the dressing room when we were back there getting her keys. My two friends were in the VIP most of the night, so after getting high with Scarlett and talking about Greek mythology in her tinted-window Honda Civic, I sat at the bar with my arms crossed while a group of construction workers joked about me in Spanish. At the end of the night, Yolanda started screaming at the manager while paying out, and she was fired. I somehow had three hundred dollars when we got home. That night, some other girls from the club came over to smoke, and we all talked about how much we had made that night, and it wasn't in a weird, competitive way.

Did you start out in a line of sex work you thought you would want to continue in, or were you treading water and learning with a plan to change it up? Club-jumping counts here. Can you talk about why?
I never had an exact date for how long I wanted to be a stripper for, but I started making a lot of money very quickly because I was treating the job like a nine-to-five and still didn't understand the reasons, ideology, and dynamics behind most of my coworkers' antiwork attitudes. I went in from seven p.m. to four a.m. five or six days a week. I just started out treating it like any other job I'd had; I have always worked hard. Yolanda club-hopped constantly, but Bambi was teaching me about how to get in good with the management, who were the Korean and Russian mafia, and the more I learned, the more they trusted me, because I could drive with blow in my car, worked whenever they asked me to, and was good at talking to the undercover cops who would come in constantly because the fact that my club was essentially a brothel was an open secret.

We stayed at this place because we were making (what to me was) an insane amount of money. I started doing extras as soon as I found out that it was low-key encouraged, as long as we tipped everyone constantly and generously and followed all of the other unspoken rules. I hadn't considered quitting stripping until I was made an unrefusable offer that took me out of the club for a few years.

I always wanted to have my shit together by twenty-five, and financial security has always been a personal goal. I knew that I never wanted to do porn after hearing about Yolanda's experiences. After Yolanda was fired from the club, Bambi—who looked like a Russian Barbie—cried in Russian to one of the door guys. A few weeks later, they called and said that we could go back to work but only at the sister club, Skin, which was the most notorious nude club in west LA, and from what I'd already seen and learned at Silver Reign, I knew this establishment would change the direction of my life. I knew that I wanted to take safe, high-paying clients for as long as I was able to after a few months of stripping and learning about doing extras in the club and seeing customers outside of the club.

What are some songs that were popular or that you loved when you first started doing sex work?

At first they only played Korn for me and Lana Del Rey for Bambi. We were white and worked at racist white clubs and that was how it was during that period. Bambi learned English from black-market Three Six Mafia tapes in Russia, so she knew a lot about rap and hip-hop and got them to start playing a little more of it. The few Black dancers were only allowed to dance to EDM remixes of hip-hop songs at Skin, though.

How has sex work—the way you do it, the way you think it's perceived and understood by outsiders, and the community of sex workers you know (if any)—changed since you started?

The way I work has changed incredibly drastically over the years that I've spent being a sex worker.

When I started, the Instagram/Twitter fame-stripper-success model wasn't as much of a thing *at all*, so some of the biggest changes I have witnessed within the community have been related to the gradual process of in-person sex work becoming symbiotic with online sex work. I think there is a lot more general awareness of strippers, cam performers, and porn performers in mainstream society now as opposed to ten years ago, but the lack of mainstream attention given to full-service in-person sex work/ers belies the biases and moral panic in regard to accepting us as fully realized human beings whose lives are worth just as much as any non-sex workers.

What music do you listen to to get pumped for work?
Gucci Mane, Britney Spears, Lil Kim, Cardi B, Migos, Megan Thee Stallion, Rosalia, and certain other flamenco songs.

What do you do to relax after a bad shift or client?
Take a Xanax, drink Hennessy or Camarena tequila, talk to a friend or completely recluse, stretching ...

Do you remember your first big money purchase with sex work money? What was it? How did you feel?
The first time I remember making a big-enough-for-me-to-remember purchase was after my first night stripping. I spent forty-five dollars at Crossroads on a translucent oval purse made from frosted resin with pressed flowers suspended throughout. It had a brass clasp and chain strap with pale jade glass gem-cut beads interwoven through it. I felt in control of my destiny, owning that purse. I broke it one night, unloading the car after work (first time I learned not to use your real-life cute shit at the club). My next biggest purchase was my car, a 2014 black Kia Rio paid outright with ($17,000 in) cash I won in Las Vegas with money given to me by a friend I met in the club, in appreciation for my good company.

Do you feel like having done sex work has given you certain skills that are useful in your day-to-day or non-swing life that others don't have? What are some of them? Are there disadvantages from sex work that also come up? If there are, will you elaborate on them?
Pros/usable skills: I learned what intersectional feminism and what capitalism were from doing sex work. I learned true appreciation and respect for the absolutely endless debt we all owe Black women for every single thing they do. I've gained a much more intimate and nuanced understanding of the violence that marginalized groups of people face in general, I think.

Sex work has forced me to develop more rounded critical-thinking skills. Because of the nature of sex work and its intersections with drug use, I have experience handling overdoses and related emergencies, understand the importance of Dial soap and cotton underwear, and have learned negotiation and de-escalation strategies. I have a high distress tolerance, the ability to think on my feet, a hot bod from pole dancing, and, let's be honest, we're all better at sex than non-sex workers, who the hell are we kidding.

Cons/disadvantages due to sex work: Low trust for people; chronic injuries from constantly slamming my knees onto the stage and falling on my ass from twelve feet in the air; having been assaulted a lot, and living with the threat of probable further abuse due to my job from clientele, management, and law enforcement; at times, use of drugs and alcohol (for a long time my only prerogative was to make the most possible money at any personal and many other costs). Difficulty maintaining romantic relationships is boring but real. I do experience (to a small degree) lack of access to certain assistance, and literal difficulty getting credit in the straight world, in the words of the venerable Courtney Love.

What do you think would make sex workers' lives better or easier or safer (or all three)?
I think that decriminalizing all sex work would immediately allow for our quality of life to begin significantly changing for the better.

Do you feel like you're a part of a larger community of sex workers? In person or on the Internet?
My sense of, and participation in, community fluctuates depending on who I have to deal with, because, while I support all sex workers, I don't get along with all sex workers. I seem to have personal issues with other sex workers mainly in regard to social media. Social media has expanded my awareness of the experiences of many other sex workers as well, though. I have never had a problem with another sex worker (other sex workers may well have had problems with me and acted fake as fuck even though I didn't notice and never will) except one time, but I couldn't help that her sugar daddy wanted to date me and give me tons of money. She took it personally, though.

How do you see power dynamics play out in your community? What kind of workers are valued by other sex workers around you, and what kind of work is most valued?
I think strippers are the second-most whorephobic type of sex worker after camgirls.

If you work in a place with a manager, what are they like? What are their interactions with the sex workers they "manage" like?

My experience has been that managers are at their core racist, misogynistic, and homophobic control addicts. I take my interactions with all management from a place of knowing that, and I manipulate the situation using any influence or privilege I have to benefit myself and most other workers. (I'm not supportive of racist bitches who use their good standing with management to bully other workers.)

Do you feel involved in sex worker activism or organizing? Do you want to be?

As a novice in the realm of sex worker activism, I want to become more involved and learn more; I've been busy working.

What kind of organizing goals are prioritized by the sex workers around you?

Immediate mutual aid to Black and trans sex workers. Also, undocumented sex workers and sex workers experiencing homelessness or working outside are prioritized by some, while others are looking to further their own personal interests and have an outstanding need for attention, money, and external validation specifically disguised as flashy activism.

Regardless of whether you're involved in activism or organizing, what do you see as important goals for us to work toward?

We need to use our respective privileges, access to resources, and influence to simultaneously be addressing the reality that most sex workers are in immediate and dire need of basic resources and be taking the necessary steps as they come to get sex work decriminalized.

What do you think are barriers to achieving those goals?

We need sex work to be recognized as a valid form of labor, and laborers afforded the same rights as any other person and not discriminated against solely because of the nature of the work. In order for that to happen, the work needs to be completely decriminalized. The barriers are not impossible to overcome if we can effectively work in support of one another and engage as a community. Everyone needs to be included, which means that certain groups of us need to be prioritized and uplifted in order to even begin to create a better world for all sex workers.

How are you coping with our current reality?
I am mainly isolating and self-medicating, trying to be there for people in my life and letting them do the same for me, and taking care of my health to the extent I am able so that I can also be of service to others, because we need to depend on one another for survival right now.

What would you like to see from white sex workers moving forward? Individually and/or as a community and/or as organizers?
I would like to see a lot of public accountability. I would like to see certain platforms given away completely to the Black sex workers and organizers who deserve to be heard. White sex workers should be engaged in constant, continual reprioritization and clarification of their community involvement and personal goals, which in my opinion as a white sex worker should be: working to ensure the safety and elevation of our most vulnerable community members.

Where do you hope to be in five years? Don't let the current state of reality hold you back: what's your ideal world that you want to be living in in five years?
In five years, I would like to have stable income, housing, and health/care. I would like to be working in other communities and industries that I have always wanted to be a part of. I would like to be in a position to provide significant mutual aid to sex workers, regardless of whether I continue to work actively in this field. It would be nice to learn a hobby and maybe have a relationship at some point, pending the physical possibility of such. I definitely would like to not be smoking weed every day by the time five years from now rolls around.

Photograph by Stephanie Kaylor

What Would You Say to Other Girls Who Are Considering It?

Stephanie Kaylor

Thus, you say you are twenty-nine for a lifetime, as you said you were twenty-four for a decade before. Thus, the lover who has not once been tested begins to imagine sores ricocheting through every movement of your tongue. Thus, you are murdered and it is not considered a crime, and when it is, it is classified as *No Human Involved*. Thus, the only way in which the townsfolk feel safe with you around their children is as a ghost, a warning to ward off the could-also-be-dead. Thus, you are rendered invisible every day. Thus, you are called hypervisible. But it is never you, not even on the screen when you read the user comments one night and see the speculation: *she was so out of it, she must have been on something / hard.*

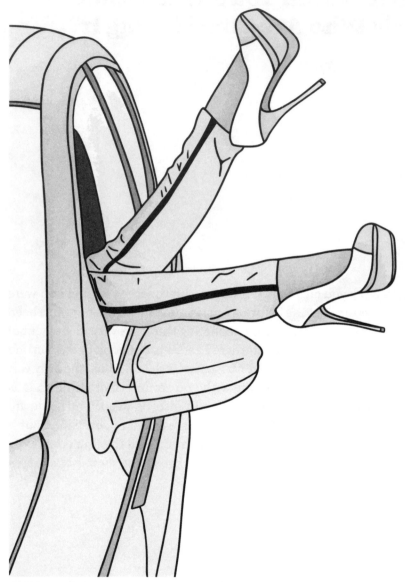

NHI, by Adrie Rose

How I Ended Up Being a Social Worker at the Veterans Administration

a conversation with Eden

Editor's Note: This conversation has been edited and condensed for length.

Between the years of 2008 and 2010, I worked at a club just outside of Fort Hood.

Can you talk more about Fort Hood?
Fort Hood is an army military base in Fort Hood, Killeen, Texas. It gained notoriety in the last several years due to multiple scandals, including the brutal murder of Vanessa Guillen, the uncovered bodies of multiple soldiers, "prostitution stings" from III Corps generals, and a mass shooting that occurred in 2009.

Fort Hood and I have a tumultuous past. During the time I danced there, Bush was replaced by Obama, who continued Bush's wars. I saw blank stares, scars, and hundreds of Killed in Action bracelets. I witnessed Black and brown soldiers struggle to reconcile with killing innocent civilians that looked like them, cringing at participating in the same systemic racism that harmed them. It was a nexus of racism, classism, feminism, capitalism, and imperialism.

There was a continuous cycle of young soldiers coming in, telling me they just wanted to talk in the lap dance area, the stuffing on those dirty brown leather couches erupting just as their tears did after a few cheap beers in our "bring your own beer" club. I absorbed their secrets, collected them like my crumpled tips.

Our greedy managers and owners blurred boundaries and walked in on us naked; they saw us as commodities. To these customers, we were therapists, though we were unqualified. We were eager to listen, stiletto legs crossed in between stage sets, sometimes sipping on drinks (mine always water), warming laps or dancing on them. Strippers are often mistaken for therapists, and where I worked we were constantly busy with a specific demographic: people with PTSD from combat trauma.

We experienced a raid one day: the pigs came in and demanded to see that we were wearing "T-backs," which are regulation double-lined thongs. This check consists of a humiliating search where we pull our thongs out and pigs shine a light to check that we are abiding by this arbitrary rule. I looked over to see a dancer being led out in handcuffs, not even afforded the time to get dressed. If she was convicted, she would become a registered sex offender and most likely lose custody of her children. She was accused of contact for simply hugging a customer during a stage set after the customer tipped her. This was normal. Luckily, the charges were dropped. Was the customer arrested? No.

I found myself growing more defiant during my last year of work. I wanted unions, I wanted change, and I wanted to help.

Two of my close friends chose jail over additional deployments. I admired them deeply and saw how difficult their decisions were. I saw more of my friends sink deeper into depression and substance use. The military did not provide the support needed for all the psychosocial stressors that were occurring, and it certainly did not acknowledge the connections of complex PTSD, traumatic brain injury, and substance use. Rather than release several of my friends from duty, the military continued to deploy them over and over again.

Can you talk more about what support there is for soldiers and vets? I know it's really minimal, but I want to get a better idea of how minimal and inadequate it is.

Support for soldiers can vary. The mental health services available within the military are scarce and inevitably focus on combat readiness and support to maintain the mission. The counselors, if civilians, are usually pressured to keep service members within their current role. If they push to medically discharge, they are often met with resistance. Service members can opt to seek community support; however, it is tricky, and if they need a higher level of care, this is reported to their command and can impact their careers. For veterans, support usually involves the Veterans Administration, or, if they have private insurance, there are community agencies, mental health providers, etc. If they don't have private insurance, there are community support organizations, Vet Centers, nonprofits, and some support groups that are free as well. There are some therapists that offer free services.

During my last year dancing at Fort Hood, I began working at an abortion clinic and became even more incensed. I continued to have club regulars reach out to me, reminding me that things were worsening. I felt helpless, and at that time, the only degree I had was a bachelor's in political science. I wrote letters to Congress, reached out to nonprofits, but nothing changed.

In 2011, I decided to begin my master's in social work. I felt my political views, specifically my antiwar stance, would enable me to serve a wide swath of the military population. I was the daughter of a deceased disabled veteran, and many members of my family had served. I decided I wanted to work for the Veterans Administration, despite all of its issues and faults. Unfortunately, due to the price of the private program and a plethora of unfortunate circumstances, I had to take a break and found myself resuming my MSW again in early 2014 while working in refugee resettlement.

I completed my master's in social work, obtained my licensed master's in social work, and began working as a social worker in an inpatient psychiatric program with individuals who had survived systemic trauma. I began applying to work with the military population and found the process was extremely grueling. During my time as an inpatient social worker, I was able to occasionally work on the military unit, where soldiers were "voluntold" to come to this inpatient program. I ran groups when they needed additional help. Many of the soldiers refused to speak; several told stories of attempted suicide and indicated they were not receiving the help they needed on base. These were not just members of the army; these were marines, sailors, and members of the air force. Nothing had changed in the years since I had left dancing; in fact, it sounded as though things had worsened. Individuals disclosed they were waiting in warrior transition units for years and that they felt useless. They informed me that their "counselors" offered nothing in terms of support, and it did not appear that there was much evidence-based practice or trauma-informed care happening. Many had just been sent to get clearance before another deployment.

Several of my friends have asked me over the years how I'm able to reconcile my political beliefs as an anti-Zionist, anti-imperialist Jewish woman with my job. I remind them that the military population is more complex than that. There is nuance in everything, and while these individuals may not have been on the occupied side of the military-industrial complex, this was a decision they made in order to make ends meet because capitalism stood in the way, and those posing that question to me and so many others aren't able to provide another solution.

Working with veterans has allowed me to use my academic experience and my work as a stripper to be a trauma-informed provider, in addition to someone who maybe "gets it." No, I don't know what it's like in a combat zone, and no, "I wasn't there!" What I understand is being marginalized and discarded and having the majority of the American population forget you exist. I understand being fetishized and glorified at times and spit on at others. There can be a similar trauma. There can be a shared "fuckedupedness" from trauma, as many of the girls and I have discussed.

Postscript (September 17, 2021)

In the weeks leading up to the withdrawal of Afghanistan, as the media continued to drown us in images of soldiers holding babies, I realized I no longer agree with my previous sentiments: I was holding on to ideals that were privileged, at best. Our military is a tool of colonialism and imperialism; it has no parallel to sex work. If anything, many of the most vulnerable who engage in sex work often find themselves on the violent, invading end of colonization. Assault and murder of local sex-working and non-sex-working women at the hands of military members come in tandem with imperialism. Military members are glorified through a colonial lens, a saviorism that is palpable for those who engage in white supremacist, imperialist, patriarchal beliefs—many of those who also link sex work to sex trafficking.

I found myself less able to defend the population I served, growing increasingly angry about the choices to engage in murder, torture, and rape overseas. The "poverty draft" became a flimsier argument as I watched more and more individuals choose other options over the military and even more choose jail over war crimes. While I had close friends who were veterans, I knew that none of them were able to reconcile with Afghanistan or Iraq or the occupations. I felt like a hypocrite. Who was I to criticize people in the military while I worked for a government organization simply for health care and the federal student loan forgiveness program. I also don't believe as a social worker that I have any right to judge anyone's life choices, because of my own.

I guess you can say that while many things are nuanced, engaging in colonialism isn't. While there are circumstances that might lead one into the military, you cannot escape the reality that sex work is a nonviolent, consensual act while military service is a violent, colonial, imperial, nonconsensual act of war and terror. Yet sex workers are demonized in a way that is acceptable and even joked about. We are dehumanized in a way that is playful and cute. We are memes and afterthoughts, while the military is glorified and worshipped, no matter what damage is done, no matter the torture or rape or pillage.

I can't help but realize I am a hypocrite.

Scooter, by peech breshears

What Did Sex Work Take from You—and How Can You Get It Back?

peech breshears

Editor's Note: The names in this essay have been changed.

Working in "the trades," as some sex workers call it, took something from me. For years, I've tried to figure out: what I lost and when, how I could get it back, and, years later, wondering if I had ever truly had those things at all. They weren't tangible things like money, clothes, or cars. Instead, I realized they were the deep things that slip through our fingers like sand before we even know we've had them (or have a chance to dig down inside it and enjoy them). I didn't have trust or faith in humanity, I had trouble making friends and keeping jobs, and I was always stressed and sick—watching my health circle back around to me for a few precious moments before being knocked back down on my ass by some new and frightening situation. I couldn't ever seem to think about people normally and found myself always waiting for the moment when a person would show me who they were and try to con me for money, sex, or whatever else it was they wanted from me. I never believed ... I couldn't believe someone would ever want me for me.

It was devastating how many times I would secretly fear people and what they might do to me, because I'd abuse myself for not trusting people, not believing the best of them—and then they'd turn around and do the very things, the harmful and hurtful things, I'd suspected they might do anyway.

Let me tell you a story about a man named Will.

I'm lucky enough to ride a Vespa motorbike. When I worked sex, it was my dream purchase: a brand-new, shining motorbike with zero miles on it until I rode it off the showroom floor. I'd always wanted a pink one—and I wanted a fast one. I'd owned a Honda Metropolitan before as well as a Chinese-brand scooter called a Q-Link (she was baby pink and named "the Piglet" because the joke was that it was a mini "hog"), both of which were 49 cc and wouldn't go over thirty-five miles per hour even if you were rolling downhill . . . on oil . . . with the wind blowing at your back . . . and a bigger motorcycle actually pushing you. They were wonderful bikes for zooming around the city, picking up prescriptions or small items from the grocer, but they weren't motorcycles. I was never going to be able to ride them farther than ten or twenty miles in a trip, and I certainly wasn't going to be able to hit a highway for any reason other than being strapped to a trailer that was being towed by a truck. So, while I struggled to make ends meet by working in a salon during the day and trading sex at night, I dreamed about a day when I'd be able to afford a Vespa. I'd dropped out of college and every month got phone calls threatening to disconnect my utilities or evict me from my home. I never had a spare dime and could never quite figure out how to survive on my own and get my bills paid. So, I struggled, prayed, cried, and worked as hard as I could to make life work for me. I was beyond broke, and a ten-thousand-dollar motorbike was a dream so expensive I couldn't even afford to have it more than a few times a year. But, in the years since, God decided to answer my prayer when I was ready for it. I wouldn't have been able to afford the upkeep, to keep it in a garage, to take care of it the way a luxury item should be taken care of—not then, I wouldn't have. But later, when I was, it happened. Now I ride a canary-yellow Vespa 300 GTS Super, and I call her "Le Bumblebee." When people tell me how cute it is and ask me why I gave it that name, I laugh and tell them, "Because I'm just buzzing all over the place! Wave at me when you see me on the highway," and I feel like a million bucks. Not a day goes by when I don't see my Vespa (or even just the helmet if it's a day I'm not riding) and say aloud, "Dear God, thank you for blessing me!" I'm telling you this because I want you to know how much I value this thing, this possession, this blessing—and why.

Before we get on to Will, we have to go back to the things I lost while I was working in the sex trade. I started at twenty-two, living in Salt Lake City, Utah, and, coming from Oklahoma and Kansas, I was not at all prepared to pay over two thousand dollars per month in rent and utilities. I'd complained to enough friends enough times that one finally said, "Why don't you just do phone sex? You've got a great voice, you don't have to sleep with anyone, you get paid weekly, you make a ton of money, and you work whenever you want!" This, to me, sounded like perfection. It sounded too good to be true, sure. But it also sounded like complete and total freedom.

Have you ever thought—deeply thought—about what the word *freedom* means? It's such a funny word, one that doesn't need to be defined. Simply by being human, we somehow innately understand the idea, the need, the want of possessing it. It's a deep, visceral understanding of both the word and the actuality of it: to live a life unencumbered by something. Bosses, responsibilities, bills, and even to some, consequences. It's beyond just wishing we didn't have to be constantly connected to clock-in machines, time cards, and printed weekly schedules; it's the imagination of floating through life, unfettered by anything other than those things we instinctively believe would finally fulfill us. Freedom isn't "not having a job," it's working at something designed to fulfill you.

I always wondered how certain people could be happy in particular vocations. My parents are completely fulfilled being Christian ministers. My husband is totally happy being an office drone with a fancy title like "network engineer." My younger brother has zero problems working hard in a factory that makes plastic items sold in big-box stores around America. Me, though? I have never felt fully satisfied doing anything that requires me to adhere to a schedule, clock in "on time," or watch whether I've tried to clock in three minutes early or clock out more than seven minutes late. While some baristas might not mind that at all and, because they are busy truly enjoying the making of two hundred "mocha-latte-mericanos" a day, never give a single thought to reading the next week's schedule again and again and again ... and again, I'm personally filled with such a deep dread at even the thought of it that words cannot begin to describe it.

For over twenty years, I styled hair and created stunning nail art. I studied, practiced, and worked all the hours I wanted—sometimes going sixteen hours a day at my nail table or behind the chair. It afforded me the opportunity to float wherever I liked, have cash in my hand at the end of the night, and never have to engage in "being coached" or knowing that some wrong decision I'd made (according to whatever a micromanaging boss would have considered wrong, even if we saw it differently) would later be termed a "teachable moment" right before I had to sign a "verbal warning." Sex work was much the same: it was a form of freedom for me that, until that moment, I had never lived the reality of; I had only dreamed it until then. I had my own personal fantasies about being a successful sex worker: consistent cash flow; the ability to turn away jobs, opportunities, and clientele; and the knowledge that I would be free.

But then, the questions come up again: What is freedom? Can we ever really be free? Sure, I never had to punch a time clock to trade sex, but I was tied to constantly checking my payment apps, worrying about legalities, being stuck on a phone day in and day out, and navigating the stigma that came along with being outed by friends and family who I'd trusted with the truth of my life and my job. I was trapped in the cycle of never knowing when the next influx of cash would happen, expanding my business to multiple streams of income to try to make ends meet, and navigating the work-life balance that included regularly being triggered into reliving many truly horrific moments from my personal life due to requests from callers, customers, and clients. Sure, I didn't have a micro-managing boss to remind me that I'd taken an extra unaccounted-for three-minute bathroom break, but I was forced to tap-dance around dealing with men and women who desired things that actively harmed me as a human being. So, where was the freedom?

I'd thought for many years that maybe someday I'd write a book, that maybe that's where the freedom would be found: a sizeable advance, a meaty and salacious topic that would get people excited to read and share, and most of all, the ability to help other people considering the sex trade as a viable way to earn money and survive. I'd always wanted to tell people the truth: it's a pyramid scheme, really. Sure, you don't have to pay in or regularly buy products to be a part of the group, but it does mirror an MLM in that so few people ever make any consistent and large amounts of money at it that the question also must be posed: is this even worth my time?

There were many, many moments when the realization would jump in my face (before I squashed it down again) that I could have made the same amounts of money, maybe even more, clocking in at a fast-food

place and serving burgers and fries. I could have made more money waiting tables, tending bar, or babysitting. I knew that, deeply. I was well
aware of it. But still, the need for freedom called me to keep dreaming,
to keep deluding myself, to keep pushing for that golden ticket–the pot
at the end of the rainbow.

So, what *is* freedom? Is it a pipe dream? Is it simple nihilism to say,
"We are not free and we never will be," or is there something else we
haven't examined yet? Is freedom–real, true, tangible freedom–possible,
or is it just a beautiful daydream?

After almost a decade of not trading sex, I've realized that trading
sex is just like any other job: you're beholden to someone, somewhere,
somehow. The freedom is there, though. It's in the consideration of the
fullness of it. It's in adjusting our views to see the situation from every
side, not just the one where we think about how much money we're
going to make, how many times we won't have to clock in anymore, or
how to deal with workplace bullying, racism, sexism, sexual harassment,
or wage inequality.

But back then, at twenty-two? I didn't know any of this stuff. All
I knew was that I needed money and I was willing to do anything to
get it. I'd grown up with two parents who worked retail jobs while they
attended seminary in Broken Arrow, Oklahoma. In fact, the money was
so tight, we'd had a car repossessed, my parents were getting a goodly
portion of our food from food banks and the day-old bread store, and my
mother eventually had to stop attending school in order for my family
to afford to have my father finish his studies. We weren't homeless,
displaced, or hungry, no. But we were struggling every single day–and
that's what I'd come to know as My Normal. Living in Utah and being
poorer, while it was stressful, wasn't much different than my perception
of my early teenage years in Oklahoma.

What differed between those times was my ability to make my own
choices. As a twenty-two-year-old woman, I could choose to secretly be
a phone sex operator at night. None of my family lived near me, I had a
cell phone for those who needed to contact me and so the number of
the landline telephone that the company required contractors to have
was private, and I had no friends or loved ones who would ever show
up unannounced and knock on my door. I was free to make whatever
decisions I needed to, and having lived through some truly harrowing
experiences as a child, and later as a teen, the concerns I had were about

physical survival—not mental or emotional, and not at all spiritually. I cared only about what I could see, taste, touch, and have—and what I considered was the easiest way to make sure I always had all of those things. To me, it was things that symbolized freedom: a house built into the side of a mountain, millions of dollars spread out over several accounts in various banks, and cars that cost more than I'd seen, heard of, or would ever make in a year.

What happened during that time, though? What about sex work was so big and all-encompassing as to change me deeply and forever? What about trading sex had required me to give away so many parts of me? It was almost like quietly and surreptitiously, the universe had snatched these beautiful parts away, leaving only an anxious, fearful, and depressed pile of human in the place where I had once stood: energetic, outgoing, and completely in love with life. I'd never had problems intro- ducing myself to people, connecting with them, even joining groups of strangers at a concert or bar and making friends for the evening. I didn't sleep all day and stay up all night staring at a television, vacillat- ing back and forth between masturbating and crying. I'd never spent the lion's share of my time wondering what life was for anyway—or why I was here in it. Those kinds of things had touched my life: true sadness, deep depression, nihilism, and thoughts of suicide and death, sure. I'd felt them, but I hadn't lived with them, hadn't given them my space—hadn't given them myself. Somehow in between the struggle to survive and the need to navigate the daily trauma I was putting myself through by working sex, the things I was losing became the things I lost. I couldn't trust people anymore; talk to thirty people a day, find out twenty-nine of them are masturbating to pedophilic rape fantasies, and see how quickly the ability to trust people flies out of the window. I couldn't make friends; the lovely couple I just met at the bar, were they actually decent people or were they also sexual abusers? I couldn't believe anyone; every sex worker I'd ever met was busy crowing about how much money they made and how sweet life was on their social media sites, but when we talked in secret, the truth was that they hated their lives just about as much as I did mine. They struggled for money, were isolated and always alone, and often comforted themselves with drugs, alcohol, or indiscriminate sex. Soon it became that I couldn't leave the house. Instead of trying to meet people, I sold pictures, videos, and webcam shows.

I lived like this for years—enveloped and suffocated by these feelings of hatred for myself—and still, I continued the trade. I was lost, flailing in an ocean of people who saw me but didn't care, recognized my desperation but couldn't be bothered, or pitied me but were focused on their own lives. The few people who saw and wanted to help me came back, over and over again, but I wasn't ready to have anything better in my life. I thought I wasn't worthy of it. I felt like a fly in a bowl of milk: extremely visible, incredibly disgusting, and now completely ruined.

I was hollow. I was a zombie.

So, I moved away. I went to school. I left the trades. I lived a life. I've been living a life all these years, trying to find what I lost, trying to get something—hell, anything—back. I married a man, got laid off, got fired, quit, got laid off again, and on and on the circle keeps rolling. This thing and that thing and then something else. But I still keep dreaming of my freedom.

And then, two weeks ago, I met Will. We found each other in a local Facebook group for people who ride Vespas. I was excited to maybe meet a friend. I'd already been on a ride with a few other people from the group and they were all Very, Very Decent people, so while I took precautions to give names, dates, times, and addresses to my loved ones, I still went out to meet Will at his house. When I arrived, it was a run-down neighborhood and I was immediately wary for myself and my bike, but Will put me at ease. He's an older man, maybe in his early sixties. He survived some disease with a lengthy name I can neither spell nor describe, and it showed from the moment I met him. He's bone-thin, his skin is pocked and peeling, and he is constantly and gently shaking. But we talked; I started by trying to make jokes, and he started by insulting me. At first it was asking me how I could "be so stupid" as to not get gas in my Vespa at the place he gets his gas. Then he moved into asking me about my bike and why I was "so simple" as to not know about aftermarket modifications like crash bars and windscreens (which is a pretentious and completely Vespa owner thing to call a windshield). While it bothered me, I knew the ride was happening and there wouldn't be much talking when the bikes started, so I stayed.

And sure, I can sit here and claim some nonsense and tell you I just didn't give a fuck and I wanted to ride, but the truth is, I wanted a friend. I wanted to trust another person and have that trust be rightly placed. I wanted to say, "*See*! There are great people in the world! I have a friend!"

So, we rode and happened upon eight young men who were riding sport bikes (BMWs, Hondas, Ducatis), and Will suggested they let us ride with them. I was shaking in my boots. I was afraid to approach strangers, but he did it with such aplomb that I couldn't do anything but let it happen—and we ended up going on a multicity ride with these guys. They were honestly really wonderful people. One of them, Lee, who has become a sort of acquaintance, said, "Now, when we leave you behind, we'll wait for you at the gas station in that little town, okay?"

I laughed and said, "When? Not if? *When*? What you trying to say!"

"I said what I said," he replied, and laughed again. "When we leave you behind!"

But we rode anyway—and they did indeed leave us behind. As soon as the highway turned into a straightaway, they sped off, doing wheelies and kicking up dust, and I thought for sure that's the last I'd ever see of them—but I comforted myself, saying it had been fun and there had been some laughs and it had felt like, just for a minute, I had some friends. Will and I got lost on some back roads, had to backtrack completely to the starting point, and had to turn around again because we'd decided we were going to ride all the way out there, even if those guys weren't there when we arrived. It would be a fun ride—and it was really fun. There's nothing quite like the wind in your face at seventy miles per hour, weaving through cars when you need to and enjoying the view as you speed by it. So, we rode. We finally got there, me taking it a little slower because Will's Vespa doesn't have the same motor mine does. His goes, but it doesn't get up and go like mine does—and that's okay. If it's two wheels and it rolls, you're good with me.

We stopped in the local Walmart parking lot, and after we'd taken our helmets off and he'd bummed a smoke from me, Will said, "I don't like those guys. They're trashy. They're trash. Did you see them doing wheelies and speeding? Weaving in and out of traffic? That's not what Vespa people do. We are classy people. I hated those guys. They are trash."

I said I thought they were cool. (Because they were fucking cool, okay? They rode fast and hit wheelies and all wore ATGATT: All the Gear All the Time. They were cool.) And again Will said I was stupid. He said something about how my Vespa wasn't as impressive as he thought it was going to be and it wasn't that special anyway to be so expensive. I laughed it off, finished my smoke, and said I was going to ride across the street and get a cold drink before heading home. I'd had it, honestly. I'd had enough of his shit to last me a day's worth of life, and I was ready to go home. So, we agreed to scoot across the street to a Taco Bell, and on our way we passed a gas station—where all of the guys from before were screaming and waving at us. Lee yelled loudest, screaming, "We've been here for an hour!"

It turned out they actually had been waiting about twenty-five minutes and had just sat there to relax until we came around. We shared stories, I told them about us getting lost, we laughed a ton, and then they invited us to go eat lunch with them at some Hooters-esque place for chicken wings. I immediately said yes, because friends, and was absolutely amazed that Will, after not four minutes earlier having called them all trash, said he would like to go along as well. I thought to myself, "I thought you hated these guys. I thought they were trash. Now you want to go eat wings with them?" but I didn't say anything at all. I just watched and noted it all in my heart.

We rode back and the guys kept a circle around me, not leaving me behind anymore. We played a game where I'd circle my index finger up and point at someone and they'd pop a wheelie. We nodded and rode and smiled and just … enjoyed life. Will pulled up the rear, and as soon as we arrived, he lit into me.

"You're stupid! You're a shitty Vespa owner! The way you were riding, it was classless. It was nasty! How could you ride that way? Don't you think any better of yourself?"

What was notable was that he made sure to do it when it was only him and me—not when the guys or my husband (who met us there) were within earshot. I noted this, how many times he called me stupid or simple. I took note of how many times he called someone trash or trashy. I took note of how horrible his reviews of people were and noticed that the nicer someone's bike was, the worse shit Will talked about them.

But I still gave him a chance. When I recounted the story of meeting him to my family, they pooh-poohed it, saying, "He … he doesn't sound cool," but I pooh-poohed them in return! I was so desperate to have a friend that I told them things like, "Ah, he's just from a different culture," and "He was probably nervous," but I knew. I knew he was a piece of shit, but I was willing to get kicked around so I could have a friend. Even after all this time, I'm still so used to the abuse and shame that comes from working sex that entering into a relationship in which abuse and shame are at the center doesn't feel so very wrong. I can find ways to justify it. I can find ways to ignore it. I can make it okay.

But then Will started asking me for money, taking my smokes out of my bag and my bike without asking me first, and even stopped us at an expensive coffee shop on what was actually only our second ride together, where he ordered the most expensive drink available and then told me, "You're going to have to get this. I left my wallet at home," before walking away and sitting at a table with his feet up.

There's more to the story, but it doesn't matter because it's all the same: it is the consideration of the fullness of the situation in its relation to my freedom that gives me pause and is the reason I'm telling you this right now. Today, in a gas station parking lot, Will screamed at me, "Fuck you. You're a piece of shit and your bike is a piece of shit. You don't even have a windscreen, you stupid little bitch. Fuck you. Get the fuck out of my face."

This would have been our third ride.

I laughed at him. I put on my helmet, threw a casual insult over my shoulder, and laughed my way out of the parking lot. While riding, I thought on all he'd said: that I was crazy, I needed to take a Xanax because I was out of control, I was bipolar and he could tell, I was poor because I don't have a "windscreen" or crash bars, I'm trash and so is my husband, and more. I thought about it, and I realized two things:

1. He wasn't really talking about me, he was talking about the things he fears people actually think about him, and
2. I didn't lose the ability to trust people, I lost the ability to
    a. trust the right people,
    b. focus on them when I meet them, and
    c. walk away from the wrong people immediately.

Those are the sobering results of years' worth of what happens when a person lives steeped in complete desperation and the struggle to survive. You can't just walk away from someone who is telling you they're willing to pay your price for whatever service you're offering when the only other option is being evicted or having your electricity disconnected in the middle of summer. You can't be discriminating in who you trust when the only other option is sleeping in your car or going without food again.

So, today, I'm thankful for Will. I'm thankful not for his abuse, but that because he abused me, lied to me, and tried to steal from me and run a short con in bad style, I had an opportunity to think about things a little differently than I normally do—and I had the ability to do that and share it with you. The question—and the answer to it—aren't black-and-white issues. It's not straightforward, and it's not easy to understand how a few years' worth of experience could or would affect a human so deeply and so strong for so long. It's deep and multifaceted. It's nuanced and fragile. That's what I tell myself when I think back on my days in the sex trades and what I lost to that work: Be gentler. Be kinder. Be easier on yourself.

Lord knows there are enough people like Will in the world. You don't need to be a Will to yourself.

love is for suckers, by xaxum omer

first, last, my only

xaxum omer

my mother's first caller has the thickest southern accent. he describes his hair as "auburn," a simple word that becomes suddenly too elegant lost in his drawl. a voice i remember, always, my mother's first john.

no matter what his name is, call him john in your heart.

i imagine the hair on my mom's first john, straight and thick like my third grade crush, amy, whose father shows up shirtless, beer in hand, and slaps her into his rusted scraper, a car made of several worse cars. amy's hair is dirty blonde, dishwater blonde. chopped to her chin for the lice then chopped again to but an inch, even when anyone can tell she cut it herself and the lice remain, even when amy stops coming to school, still her hair is the perfect dirty dishwater blonde. dark eyes, too young to be so purple underneath over so many freckles, sunspots in my memory. it hurts when she smiles. i give amy's perfect hair and the haircut she'd given herself the last time i saw her to my mother's first john. i may even give him her homey warm smell of urine, beer stains on the same flower pattern dress every day, slaps in the backseat of her father's car.

i gift john a long chin, no lips, dark pink papercuts under a hook nose, aquiline but too poor to take the compliment. i make him dark. i can tell by his voice that he is not the dark that my mother and i are, black, glowing ash, sin of the earth. he was made dark by work, the smell of outside, sun, something only a landholding away from our poverty. i make john dark as light can be. i can't make him quite as dark as we are. no one can.

we giggle as he describes himself. so new, i'm eleven, she's thirty-five, mother and child, but there, in our bed whose width is almost that of our entire small studio, we are the same, two fresh giggling whores. it's easy to laugh now. it doesn't hurt yet.

my mother's first john says he lives on a farm, he has no friends or lovers. when he is in need he fucks one of the goats or chickens. chicken feels better, but is harder to catch and makes distracting noise. goats are slower, more to hold, an easier, softer lay, their moaning something more akin to how a woman's love might sound. it is all funny until he says he's never made love to another human, never touched a woman other than his kin. in sadness john becomes familiar.

every john has at least one sadness. a smart whore finds it, dances for it, whispers sweetly, sucks, spits, rubs it till it shines. a smart whore knows what sadness is for.

a woman limps behind a walker under a matted wig in black faux adidas stretch pants, a sports bra, and a scowl. one leg won't bend, a scowl wills her forward when the leg won't. wrinkles, sagging skin, melted makeup– everything is falling apart but her tits. i smell my mother on the breeze.

the company that ships calls to our tiny room gives my mother a book. i call it the whore bible. xeroxed, one sided, old school font from a computer with a black screen, yellow text, and a blinking yellow cursor. an alphabetized list of things phone whores need, mostly slang for sexual acts and fetishes. i flip through, scanning, curious, eager.

she wakes me, whispering,

"what is cbt?"

i pop alive, upright, thumb the bible, alphabetical.

"cock and ball torture. he wants you to hurt his nuts, probably with high heels."

she thanks me, whore to whore, and tells me to go back to sleep, mother to child. the boundaries between whore and mother are as flexible as a street walker's hips.

john asks, "what do you look like?"

whore asks, "what do you want me to look like?"

she needs me, another whore, to moan on the phone while she takes a pee. she becomes my first pimp, gently. there is no force needed when there is no choice. she is what she needs to be to take care of us, i am what i need to be to take care of her. the mercurial nature of identity in the world of sex for sale

which is the whole world.

i've never seen anybody put their hands on my mother. i don't know it's possible for my mother to be hurt.

i wake up, the lights are on. my sensitive mother never turns the lights on at night, barely turns them on during the day. waking up in the middle of the night to lights on in our home i figure someone has died or worse. i am right.

we live in a one bedroom apartment. we've just come from living in our car, not for the first time or the last. the living room is large, my mother sections part of it off with a roll out bamboo divider to create my room. i love how beautiful she makes our home when she is able to make our home.

i stare at the ceiling, looking for an answer to why it is so bright in our home, which loves so much to be dark. more and more awake now i hear sound, human sound i do not know, cannot name. i do not want to get up. i know this is no good.

i walk to the other side of the bamboo.

here is my beautiful mother, her undertones glowing red in the light. she brought that couch back with us from korea after her stint in the reserves. we've had it since we lived in tacoma. we've lived so many places, very few things have stayed with us. the couch matches the papasan chair, i love them both for being old and ours. rare. here is my mother on the couch, our couch, with a man on top of her—no

yes—his hands are around her neck, this is not right. her hands are holding his wrists. i see strain, see through her skin, veins, tendons, into the body that made me, earth that grew me, the mountain of her, my first love, most beautiful. this man is choking my god. her eyes squeeze tight, as if shutting them hard enough will pull her beyond whatever this is. what is this. i see tears, but the tears and i do not know what is going on.

"what are you two doing?"

he lets go, gets off of her. she gasps, puts her own hands where his just were.

"go back to bed."

one voice, unison.

i go back to bed.

my mother tells me the truth all my life, even things i do not need to know. she offers me the most of herself, even what i am not fit to receive. i never ask about this night. she never tells.

my mother is stronger than L, she could easily fling him off. this is *our* home, we finally have that, she could put him out, call the cops if he refuses. it makes so little sense that i do not question it. in thirty years since then i have yet to see that woman weak. this night i see something worse than weakness, worse than death: a strong woman not using her strength.

one day i have a child and understand why strong mothers let weak men strangle them: to keep from waking the baby, letting the children see the truth, that some men say "i love you" with hands clenched too tight around the neck, and some women love only, exactly, those men.

one day i find myself pretending to be weaker than a weak man. i find answers to all the questions i never ask, buried in my body.

we drive to meet a man. i figure it's the flake who said he'd take us skiing then bailed. i love skiing, my father took me once. he takes his real family every year. i want very badly to ski with my real family. i chomp at the bit to ask why i've been denied, to see if he's just another coward scared to meet the child of the woman he's fucking. we find L playing basketball.

"how's your knee?"

"my knee?

"yeah, your knee."

"fine. hurt it balling in college but it's good now."

"then why didn't you take us skiing?"

i read lies, i read truths, all praise the divine gifts of trauma. i read two things on L's face:

1. he has no idea what i'm talking about.

2. i am in huge trouble.

rule, when your single black mother is dating:

do not ever mention one man to another.

EVER.

my life is in this man's hands. i explain that i thought he was some-one else, and that my mom will be pissed if she finds out i slipped.

i brought you into this world
i can take you out
"please don't tell."
L says he won't. i look into his eyes, hold out my hand.
"shake on it."
how my mother taught me, eye contact and a handshake, the next best thing to a signed document. we lock eyes, shake hands. i trust him.

when my mother says that he told, she's not even mad. that too, seems wrong. it's not that he lied, it's that his lie rang true.

i stay up all night trying to convince her, a night i remember too well—every time it hurts, for the next decade, she recalls that night.

"you were right. i should have listened."
she will never listen
this is not the first time
this will not be the last
there is no first time
there is no last

years later, living in the car again, again she holds me too close and drops hot tears into my hair and eyes. it gets cold so fast, the spittle of regret. she says,
"i'm sorry."
i hate tears. i hate
"i'm sorry."

K is a big bitch. shiny, dark, six feet, broad, a refrigerator with a round face, low tits, broad hips, and a sweet gut. she's beautiful to me now, in memories. not then, too big, saying things that make no sense, that the first people were women who conceived without men, that men are useless—my mother could never. K is a woman empowered by her identity as a whore, proud to run men's pockets, pretending to be young, thin, petite, and white. K's pride is matched by my mother's shame. two poles, axes of my world.

K never fucks or even meets her men in person, she uses whore magic over the phone and they send money. now, i see K was a genius. then, all of it seemed too good to be true. no one in my world ever said that any woman, especially a dark skinned, big bodied, older single mother, deserved to live well off of lying to men. K seemed like a fraud.

"it's easy, girl."

K was another single black sex working mother. she tried to help us.

funny how getting paid to not fuck is more shameful than fucking for free.

one day we come home and the front door to our apartment is open. my mom goes in, tells me to wait. will she come back out? i cry. when i see her again she is pouring through an awful mask of pain, all red, nose tip glowing, all wet, shining, still beautiful. the mountains rain, god cries.

my mother's room is tossed, the slashed waterbed cries with us for the plants upended, soil in the carpet, phone ripped out of the wall, doors torn from the hinges. L. he's gone, still i see him in the wet of the carpet, the sound of my sobbing or is it my mother or is it the still dripping waterbed.

we can't call anyone. this mess decides who we are, shows us to whom we belong, leaves us with no voice to disagree. L is very good at this. he knows how to make oceans pour out from god and all the mountains.

one day you're sitting on your bed doing whatever kids like you do after school, before the tired mothers come home. L knows you are home alone. he comes to you in your mother's tall and tan bamboo, grabs you by your feet, drags you twice across the length of the carpet, says something about how you should go live with your father, and leaves.

you have rug burn from shoulder to shoulder, ass to neck. fire for flesh.

you'd been playing with L's daughters, holding B's legs while C tickled her. B got rug burn on her back. it was an accident.

B is younger than you, smaller, colorful barrettes and balls in her hair. she looks like L if he were innocent, sober. you love her, she makes up for the siblings you don't see, your father's real family, your family that is not real. B has to share her father with other children, other women. B is like you, you would never do anything to hurt her. you tell C's mother you are so sorry, crying. C is L's daughter by another mother, also younger and smaller than you. you love them the way you would love to love your siblings who are not real.

B & C make you a big sister again. B & C are your real family *aren't they?*

C is shaking. C is older than B and always shaking, like L, but she's not a drunk so it makes no sense even though it makes perfect sense. C tells her mom,

"we were just playing, it was an accident."

C's mom has always been kind, another mother. she understands, believes C, believes you, but her face doesn't settle above the eyes. clouds hang in the mountains. she calls B's mom. you've never met B's mom. you were honest, C's mom believed you. you are a good big sister. you think everything is fine. C keeps shaking.

everything is never fine with an abuser
abusers only love victims and other abusers
which are you

i left home for school but i didn't know how to live and soon found myself back with my mother. she's working the lines again, living with a degenerate whose only value is that he owns his house. his favorite pastimes are watching porn while chatting on the phone with his mother, stretched out on the couch, and sitting outside the room where I stay, listening while i work the lines. i've just turned nineteen. my mother is bothered to live with an incestous ebophiliac, but not bothered enough to give up free rent.

every so often she gets the degenerate drunk and lets him stay over in his own bedroom to feel her tits while she jacks him off. i hear him on the phone with his mother, bragging about fucking mine, hollering over the moaning porn—he has no idea that my mom is paying rent in handjobs and blind eyes to his habit of lingering in the hallway. my stomach still turns to see shadows move under a closed door, the sound of his coarse breathing.

he doesn't know that my mother is a whore so masterful she makes you think her hand is a pussy and her manipulations are your advantage. when he threatens to kick us out, she threatens to leave. the argument ends. my mother is one of the best whores i've ever met. a real natural.

my mother doesn't force me to work the lines or hold me down when my baby's father rapes me, only that she raised me to never say no. i go to compton community college during the day, collecting financial aid, and i work the lines at night. i give all of my income to my mom, out of guilt over all i'd seen her go through. i forget that i went through it too. i owe her for raising me and she owns me.

i brought you into this world
my mother groomed me well.

you're so nervous. you sit on a black futon with none-too-mysterious white stains at an "office" in burbank, the none-too-lowkey porn capital of southern california. about twenty-five women, all latina, most of them heavyset with big bangs and no eyebrows, are sitting in cubicles wearing headsets, working calls. the woman next to you is on probation: her callers complained about her kids in the background. she is nineteen, like you, but not like you. she's just gotten her clit pierced and unzips her low cut jeans to show you, no underwear, no boundaries, no shame. her pubic mound is shaved, raw, puffy with youth, and covered in hair bumps. she has braces, rainbow colored brackets.

"what are you in for?"

she assumes you're in trouble like her. you tell her this is your interview.

"oh."

the woman interviewing you returns and hands you a booklet. triggered, giddy again, you knee-jerk, "oh, a whore bible. my mom used to have one of these." you forget to be nervous or ashamed.

"what did you say, girl? whore bible? that's funny. your mom talks?"

"yeah. she started when i was a kid."

"cool, that's cool, you'll be good at this. wanna see my hole?"

you've just seen someone else's pussy for the first time in real life and now you're being offered another? where are you? who are you?

you are at a phone sex call center sitting on a futon stained with human fluids, about to be shown another hole. you are a whore.

the interviewer lifts her shirt.

"i have to wear a fucking maxi pad over it 'cause this shit leaks."

the hole, about the size of a bullet wound, is dry and red around the edges. at least it's not another barely legal razor burned mons pubis. when she presses her fingers into either side of the hole, green pus oozes out.

"i went to mexico for lipo and the doctor left a tube in me. okay, let's see how you do on a call."

you get the job and you're happy even though you don't want any of this. your mom is waiting in the car.

"if you average over seven minutes a call for the week, that's how much you make an hour for that week, up to fifteen. eight minute average, eight dollars an hour, ten minute average, ten dollars an hour. less than seven minute average for the week and you'll be back on this couch for more training."

you never return to this couch. good girl.

she doesn't force you
    she doesn't let me choose
    i'm still a virgin
    you were never a virgin
    you were born from a whore
    i was born a whore
    my god is a mountain
    do you remember
    when the mountains cried
    i have no god

peter calls every tuesday at four, right when my shift starts. i tell him to put clothespins on his nipples and balls, shave his pubes and ass, fill his raw asshole with ice cubes, rub icy hot where he shaved, and spank himself with a ping pong paddle. he begs for permission to touch his dick, i only give it when he sounds like he's about to die, i only give it to save his life.

when he cums birds fly, waves crash, legs of light break through dark clouds. he's always so grateful, heaving,

"thank you, mistress. you're the best."

you're welcome

richard is an asshole. he knows all the girls, everyone's schedule. he intentionally calls right before shifts change so he can hold you over. control. i work four p.m. to midnight, and like clockwork, every thursday at 11:50, richard calls. i enjoy richard though, i know how to work him. i remember our first call with clarity, the raw taste of a first kiss.

richard breathes heavy into the phone, struggling for joy.

"hey baby, you there?"

more struggle

"i've been sitting here waiting for someone sexy like you–"

"No you haven't! Lying whore! You don't care about me! Nobody cares about me!"

before our first time, a moderator comes on the line to prep me.

"he's real mean. if you want me to drop in, say your roommate just got home."

i've only been working a couple weeks, most of my calls had been tame. the four-to-twelve is mild compared to the overnight. my johns are usually like peter, fetish callers who want domination, or the bored and lonely who want to complain about their girlfriends, wives, or jobs and have a sweet woman's voice to help them cum at the end so they didn't feel like bitches for emoting. i have one caller, steven, who likes me to invite my big black boyfriend over. steven likes me to "force" him to suck gigantic black cocks. at the end of every call, right after he cums, he yells, **"I'm not a fucking faggot!"**

richard is having a man-baby tantrum. i try being sweet.

"baby, why are you so upset? i just wanna spend some time with you–"

"No you don't! You're just faking it! That's all you whores do."

okay, richard. you wanna dance? let's dance.

"You called me! And for what? To be mean? I'm trying to have fun and you're ruining it! Be nice or I'm not gonna talk to you anymore!"

my hands are shaking. i don't stand up for myself. who am i? i remember the moderator is listening. shit. am i about to lose my job? my mom is gonna be so pissed–

"sorry, i'm so sorry, baby. please keep talking to me, i didn't mean it. i won't be mean, just please keep talking."

oh. i did good? okay. keep going. work him.

at forty-five minutes the system automatically cuts our calls, they call that "maxing out." i had never maxed out before richard. that first time and every time after, he immediately called back and demanded to have me again.

"do you want me to take him? you can start and we'll go to party mode so you can clock out, there's another girl he likes."

no, there are no other girls. richard is mine.

richard called every thursday at ten till midnight and maxed out at least twice for the rest of the time i worked for that service. i loved richard, still do. i love all men who pay me.

i love only men who pay me

you have one who feels so good, at least. outside time just born stars hover, blinding, forget where to begin, how to end. love him with whatever you have of love, want him in all places, on every memory, with every sin. pussy and tits, hands and mouth, asshole begging for a thumb to hold till there is cum moaning on the wall and you are nothing, nothing, and he is gone and he is nothing too, you are one. stare at it, you don't want to clean it. maybe it will bring him back. he never calls, you want him, always

or do you want him to want you

he gets you pregnant. you want to be a mother. he calls you then, every day, back to back like lovers sleep during a fight, asses touching, whenever your phone is on he is calling to tell you that you hate yourself, say you did it on purpose, cry, beg, threaten.

you didn't know why
the moon was so full

"i'll drag you to the abortion clinic myself."

he calls you more in the weeks it takes to wear you down than he did in seven years spent fucking you on the side. funny how you belong to the one who doesn't want you. funny how he never pays, but you are still his whore. funny how you can be a whore and not know it.

your child's father keeps raping you, you have no idea because you do not know who you belong to. he never feels good to your body or kisses you or stops when you ask. you say it hurts, he says you are too tight. he feels like nothing or pain, still you want him, you want it

but you don't even know what "it" is, do you? lol

"why do i have a body?" you ask no one and no one answers.

for nothing, or pain

funny how you can be someone's victim and not know it. funny how you'd rather be a victim than alone.

you've been fingered, licked, sucked, and fucked, you've been raped. no one has ever made you cum. the nineteen year old white boy whose dick you sucked when you were two made sure you were never a virgin. you gave birth before you ever made love. you sold sex before you ever had it.

child in my arms. snow, so much snow, inches, feet cover my feet, melt into my shoes. heavy child, crying, tossing, tiny beautiful frozen eyelashes.

keep going, can't stop.

child screams more, more snow falls silent.

in the mirror, the body they used to cum in. baby sleeps. numb, aching, not theirs, more and more mine. baby sleeps, slowly mother wakes. don't want to be touched, don't want to be kissed, only want to see what is left. what remains. who owns this body? who cares for it? hold it, touch it gently, no one else. this body has given so much pleasure. what can it receive? does it want? soft nipples, pale red, baby sucked the black off, dark line down the belly, fading
  take a picture, it'll last longer.

the first time i get paid for a nude photo i feel my heart throbbing in my pussy—same heart, same pussy beating as i bark back louder than richard growls, he bares his teeth but mine are sharper, i shake dust up from the earth, digging my claws in, thick pendulums of foamy saliva dangle and stretch from my jowls but never fall
  come at me bruh
  my heart beats in my panties as i hear his ears pull back. he pisses down his legs, terrified i'll leave, and in that warm homey piss puddle he belongs to me, lover, child, mother, victim, predator, phone that finally rings and all of a sudden won't stop. you belong to it because you can't ignore it and you can't make it stop, hungry dog before sizzling meat, too hot to eat, too sweet to turn away. i belong to my mother when she makes me a whore, my rapist smashing into my cervix, cum on my wall, still fetus i press out, squatting on the toilet seat, screaming, tiny chicken bones and blood soup. i belong to birth, owned by the white voices ordering me to push a child i can't rush, can't stop, curling out with the face of my rapist, dark eyes, dark hair, porcelain skin—
  how does this dark body
  give birth to such light?
  the most beautiful sight i've ever seen other than my own body, from my own body, the one that didn't die when everyone who owned it threw it away. who needs forgiving?
  now that they've thrown me away i am mine
  now that i am mine there is nothing to forgive

my son's daycare calls. i'm at school, my mom was supposed to drop him off at one o'clock. it's two. i start to sweat.

the voice on the phone asks where my child is. i say,
"i don't know. i don't know where my son is."
what kind of mother
doesn't know where her child is?
lol who are you?
you leave class and call your mom. no answer. you call your mom,
no answer. your shirt is wet, you're sweating so much, or are you crying
through your skin?
remember the mountains?
your eyes fill with boiling water, the world tilts
looks kinda cool actually
everything is wobbling, vibrating. the entirety of your flesh cries.
you smell yourself, emotions made physical, a pour. levee breaks rage,
levee breaks sorrow. you call your mom you call your mom you call your
mom like you call for milk like you call your ex for dick like your ex who
only ever calls back to drag you to abort his child
you don't know why the moon is full
until it is too late
at four o'clock your mother calls. three hours missing, two hours of
sweat. before you answer you say to yourself,
"this better be good"
lol you know it won't
"hey jess, what's up?"
she's giddy, lively. the gas is lit
i hate you lol
"Where are you where is my child"
"where are we, that's a good question—the bus broke down"
**"Okay so why the fuck didn't you call me you have my child what
the fuck Mom"**
"oh, well the baby was watching a video"
**"Are you fucking serious right now Mom I've been so fucking
scared I'm in school trying to hold my life together what in the entire
fuck"**
"wow, you really need to calm down and work on your anger issues"
you punch a wall in the hallway outside your classroom. not the
first time, not the last. you still feel it, the wall punches back, crying all
over, rage or pain? same thing?
lol if you could suck as hard as life does

you'd be a rich whore
you call a friend,
"Please stay on the phone with me"
you can't breathe, air is too thick
"So I can go get my baby without choking my mother"
you beg, not the first time, not the last
if you hit her she'll call the cops they'll take him away just pick the
baby up and walk away
"Promise you won't hang up I need you I don't want to hurt her
it's not her fucking fault I love my mom I just need to get my baby
safe please don't hang up"
don't say anything don't look at her just pick up the baby and walk
away
you cry, you sob, you shake
wow i've never been so upset before this is wild
"I have him oh my god"
hold him tight he's all you have

baby with my first pimp's eyes you are so heavy, perfect in my arms. you
have no idea what's going on my silly sweet rapist's baby. touch my face,
hold my cheeks. i love when you do that, small hand shining, wet with
tears. puts your cheek on my bare chest, it is warm, bright. tears between
us.

the last time you saw your mother it was spring, mellow breezes, mild
weather. a good day to walk down eastern parkway in brooklyn clutching
your rapist's child, sobbing with joy that he's alive and you got him back
without choking your mother to death like you wanted.

i love my mother. i miss her voice, sometimes i smell her, see her in my
dreams, become her as i become myself. i don't speak to her, don't know
where she is. i hope she's eating well. i'll never forgive her for being my
first god, first beauty, first love, my first mountain, first abuser, my first
pimp. i won't ever forgive her because there's nothing to forgive.

i saw a video a couple years ago of a worker in a corset, tits perfect creamed
gobs of wobbling, sweet hand hammering a john's glasses into the hard-
wood floor with the stacked toe of a stiletto platform. immaculate

violence and i was inspired, reminded of the body that pounded into mine to conceive my child. i said stop. he didn't. he's still going.

i keep going to stay ahead of all the men who never stop.

i've never been kissed, never made love. my rapist's son has the most beautiful face i've ever seen, eyes of the grandmother he doesn't remember. for months after that last spring, he ran after any older black woman with long braids, calling, reaching. "**Mother dear!**" he'd ask me questions about his dad, he liked when i did impressions of his father's voice, he'd laugh and laugh, beg for more. the only thing sadder than him asking me to call my first pimp or speak in my rapist's voice was when he stopped.

i don't fuck, i can't be touched. i get my rocks off selling nude photos and videos, bend my body, pull my flesh open, show the pink, whispers and lies set free. how many of my ancestors knew how to turn an empty wet spot into a full pocket?

no excuses, no apologies, nothing to forgive.

pay me. i'll fold my body, curve your sadness into joy. let me be your good whore.

"what's your name?"
   what do you want it to be?

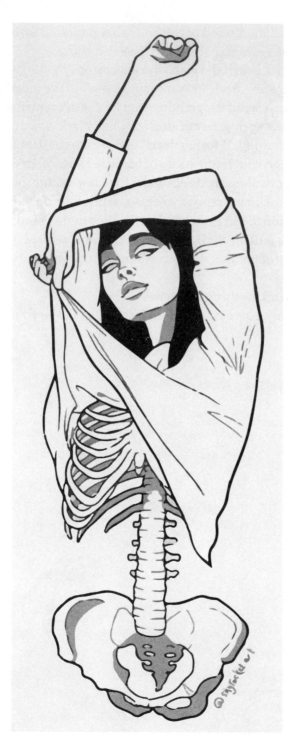

Skin, by Sky Rocket

Respectability Politics by Any Other Name: Sex Work, Sports, Service, and Therapy

Janis Luna

A little over a year ago, I was still in grad school, pursuing my master's of social work and writing for *GO Magazine* under my stripper name as a side hustle to what I guess was technically my side hustle, while my main hustle was an unpaid internship I had no choice but to participate in.[1] I went to grad school with the goal of one day becoming a therapist with a private practice. One fucked-up thing about social work school (other than the two years and 1,200 hours of unpaid work, three full days a week for two years, and fuck you, I guess, if you have bills to pay) is that sometimes they try to shame you for wanting to go into private practice— at least, a small subsection of the professors at the school I attended did, preferring, I suppose, that we all become martyrs instead and subsist on the sweet, fulfilling succor that is sainthood.

Luckily for me, I only had to hear about those professors from some of my classmates; my first professor on my first day of grad school made absolutely no bones about the fact that private practice is the bread and butter of most social workers nowadays, and any other kind of job is likely to burn you out in your first couple of months there *and* force you to kiss your ethics goodbye as you work for institutions that have been deliberately created to fit the agenda of white supremacy and capitalism.[2] That my "secure the bag" professor was a Black man is definitely not lost on me. We had our issues–he, like most of my professors and classmates, was thoroughly unaware of sex worker cultural competency practices, or that they should even be a thing[3]–but I'll always appreciate him for that.

Anyway, grad school was where I got my first experience as a baby therapist and, given the way social work school is structured, was also the time in my life when I was still a babystripper: I was barely a year into dancing when I started school at twenty-seven. Old for a babystripper, but probably the best time in my life for me to have started, so I try not to regret it too much–any earlier in my twenties, and I was a mess who didn't know her own boundaries and probably would have gotten very, very hurt.[4] I'm always in awe of young strippers who start dancing at eighteen, nineteen, twenty years old; many are taken under the wing of more experienced dancers, but many more are just tough as nails and take no shit. That was not me as a teenager or an early adult, and I needed the almost-decade I spent in health-care administration and customer-service work to toughen me up before doing the hardest and most demanding job of my life, with the steepest learning curve and the most meaningful personal results. (I'm talking about stripping here, though therapy is pretty challenging and pretty great too.)

As a stripper, and as a baby therapist, it was easy for me to conflate the two, and I wrote about it in an article for GO Magazine titled "How Being a Stripper Mirrors My Work as a Therapist."[5] In general, I don't like to go back and read my old writing; it usually serves as a snapshot of who I was at the time, and that person is usually not quite as bright and incisive as she thinks she is. I suspect that many writers who publish their work feel this way. But I went back recently, just about a year after I wrote that piece, having two years under my belt as a social work intern, four months as a staff therapist, and three full years as a sex worker, and I'm not as chagrined as I thought I might be. I say some pretty smart things about the similarities between therapy and sex work: that the relationships in both industries are explicitly transactional (and that's what helps in creating boundaries); that some aspects of interacting with a sex worker are therapeutic for some clients; and that fantasy functions heavily both in the therapy office and in the strip club, though for different ends.[6] I also lay out the similarities that sex work and therapy contain with regard to emotional vulnerability, as well as the acceptance and affirmation of so-called deviant desires for clients and customers alike. Way to go, past me.

But even then, slowly emerging from babystripperhood into stripper adolescence, it was clear to me the ways in which sex work and therapy diverge. I bring this up now because, after the release of *Hustlers* last week, conversations around what other industry sex work is like have cropped up, mostly because non-sex-working civilian movie stars are being asked questions about sex work, and I guess they have some feelings about their approximation of sex work even merely as a role.[7] While they play sex workers on TV, they don't actually know what it's like to be a sex worker.

Three years in, and I'm definitely not saying that I'm the expert; frequently, I defer to more veteran sex workers.[8] Something that my philosophy on sex work and my philosophy on being a responsible, ethical therapist both contain is valuing humility and the idea of bringing curiosity and a beginner's mind to the work. As a therapist, I apply this to my clients, who are always the experts in their own lived experiences; this is especially important in the context of sex worker cultural competency (though individual agency is something that even the most master clinicians tend to forget when it comes to working with sex workers). Within sex work, humility, curiosity, and a beginner's mind correspond to respecting sex workers more marginalized than myself: Black, queer, and trans workers; poor and outdoor so-called "survival" workers; workers with disabilities; and sex worker elders, people who have been living activism longer than I've been alive.

In the aftermath of *Hustlers*, this humility is something that I notice is very obviously absent from the civilians who donned our experiences as costumes for millions of dollars and probably at least one Oscar nom, and I would be lying if I told you it didn't chafe. For example, in an interview with NPR, Constance Wu explained that strippers use their bodies for entertainment, which is "exactly what an athlete does," and pointed out the hypocrisy in the fact that one of those jobs is stigmatized and the other is celebrated. She's not wrong, of course, but something about the comment didn't sit quite right with me. It reminded me of my own babystripper insistence that being a stripper was "like being a naked therapist." Years later, I can now recognize that the number of clients who sought me out for the therapeutic nature of my services can be counted on one hand, with several fingers left over. Put simply, most strip club customers are seeking out entertainment, usually in the form of titties in their faces and a smooth, round ass grinding over their dicks.

It was something I was aware of when I wrote that piece for *GO Magazine*, and I made sure to include it in a segment at the end of the piece: How is a stripper not like a therapist? It's pretty solid, and I spent two years and thirty thousand dollars learning how to do APA formatting, so I'm just going to include it here: Therapy is widely accepted as a legitimate form of work, while sex work is not.[9] And while a clinician's clients may sometimes develop unhealthy or inappropriate attachments to their therapists, it usually doesn't pose much of a threat to the therapist.

By contrast, some of the women I dance with have been stalked, and there's little recourse for them when something like that happens, as sex workers are often accused of "leading a guy on" (hello, creating a fantasy is literally part of our job) and are assumed to be deserving of the violence we encounter.

Finally, therapists–hopefully–pursue their work, at least in part, because they want to help people heal. Strippers are there to pay our bills, and the primary function of our job is to be an entertainer, not a shrink.[10] Providing a healing experience for someone can be a welcome, but by no means mandatory, side effect of that. More and more frequently, though, the men who come to my club are coming in with a sense of entitlement: that because I'm there, and because I'm feminine-presenting, friendly, and undressed, they're entitled to my services (conversation, entertainment, dance) for free or cheap. No one expects their therapist to work for free, even if they do find it fulfilling to provide support, validation, and guidance. It shouldn't be expected of strippers and sex workers either.

The difference between sex work and therapy, or sex work and sports, is that no one feels the need to compare therapy or sports to some other industry to clean it up and make it respectable–both of those occupations stand on their own, and no one will ask you to explain to them in detail how your daddy hurt you in order for you to pursue therapy or professional athleticism as your career (though therapists are definitely a bunch of weirdos who chose a career that allows us to ask rude and invasive questions so bluntly that society would frown on us in any other context). I also wonder, in these comparisons, exactly which sex workers are perceived to be providing therapeutic services to their clients, or which sex workers feel the need to identify themselves that way.[11] (If I had to, I would probably guess that it's white or white-passing sex workers who get coded that way, and we always have to remember that respectability politics operate along white supremacist lines more than anything else.) The same goes for athleticism, with many able-bodied dancers being sticklers for the entertainment and athleticism aspect of the work (which, come on, nobody makes that much money from the stage, and my customers could give a fuck the day that I learned how to successfully pull off Superman), leaving unathletic dancers (disabled, injured, or just not athletically inclined sex workers[12]) out in the cold. The athleticism and art of pole dance is what I use at work to work off some of the energy that comes from doing a stigmatized job for ungrateful, entitled bastards night after night, but it doesn't put a roof over my head in the slightest, to be frank.

In her interview with NPR, Wu also compared sex work to the service industry, a comparison that I consider far more apt than either therapy or professional sports. It's something that my brother, who is a bartender, and I talk about often. Having graduated from my master's program, I now work three days out of the week as a fee-for-service therapist. (I get paid the same amount for a forty-five-minute actual therapy session as I do for a four-minute lap dance, but that's a whole other story.) When I tell people that, they're mostly impressed. A stark difference from the responses I get if I tell people I'm a stripper (if I tell them at all—not everyone deserves to know that about me), or the responses I got when I was doing receptionist work, or that my brother gets from some of our family members, who often wonder what he's going to do with his life when he "grows up" as if being a bartender is not a job for an adult, and a demanding job at that. The service industry, customer service, and sex work—all of these jobs share in common a strong, unifying element of emotional and physical labor, and to some extent, that labor is even sexualized across industries, though of course it is most explicitly sexualized within the sex industry. We flirt, we suck up, we tease, we cajole, we smooth over, we grin through our gritted teeth; we sell, we sell, we sell, we sell.

I'm no longer a babystripper, and I have the sense that I'm rapidly exiting my therapist infancy: with every week that goes by, I feel more confident in my abilities in both arenas, and both jobs feel more and more different the longer I do them. The more time passes, too, the less interested I become in the respectability politics of dressing up what it is I do to provide for myself.[13] There are times when it still feels like a risk, to describe among non-sex-working colleagues what, precisely, I do for money. I don't have to go into detail, of course; it's none of their business. But I find when I don't, the narrative of stripper-as-therapist is one that gets foisted on me, usually without my consent. I'm not interested in that. Prettying things up to make other people more comfortable is not something I advise my clients as a therapist. I value authenticity and the courage it requires, and I believe that living our most authentic lives—regardless of how that may fly in the face of what is considered a respectable norm—is how we save ourselves and, by extension, each other. So no, I'm not a naked therapist. I'm a stripper at the club and a therapist at the clinic, and I'm proud of both jobs for being exactly what they are.[14]

Emily's Responses

1   Ah, the MSW-program-to-sex-work pipeline! Not only are the internships unpaid, *we are paying for them* because they count as a course. I have no idea where the money goes, as field instructors aren't paid and we aren't using university resources during those hours. I often think about a tweet that made the rounds sometime in 2019 advertising a "reverse-financed internship," where you pay to work. It was a joke, but that's actually exactly what MSW students and a lot of other students in professional grad programs do. Meanwhile, public agencies and private nonprofits could not function without MSW interns. And so those of us without family money either go into massive debt, work ourselves to death, or, well, do sex work.

2   This. It's much easier to be an ethical sex worker than an ethical social worker! Those of us with abolitionist values have to work hard to maintain them in this field.

3   *Big mood.* This seems to be the case in literally every MSW program. Watch out, we are calling from inside the house and are going to burn it down!

4   Indeed. That was my experience long before I figured out that clawing my way through grad school at the similarly advanced age of twenty-nine was probably my best long-term exit strategy. Because, well, we know how I feel about other work.

5   Hahahahaha nooooo! "*It's not therapy!*" is my favorite rant to go on. I definitely do see some parallels, though, and I also published some profoundly embarrassing takes in my baby sex worker days, so nothing but empathy here.

6   This is also very, very true in BDSM work. I specialize in role play and love thinking about the similarities and differences between the role plays dommes/subs/switches do with clients and the role plays therapists do with clients.

7   Boy, do they ever.

8   We love to hear it. Ten years and I sometimes still feel like I don't know shit.

9   That's it right there. Most everything else falls out from that—stigma, criminalization, violence. We can go into details about the differences with accreditation and between sexual labor and emotional labor (never the twain shall meet in therapy), but that's less important than the social conditions surrounding the work.

10 *Tell them!*

11 Saying the quiet part out loud here!

12 No one really knows what dominatrices do, and as a chronically ill woman I like to explain that much of it is lazy stripping: I will take off my top. I will not dance. And these shoes are coming off immediately.

13 Hell yeah.

14 Standing O.

Playtime, by Beyondeep

Beyondeep

Do you remember the first time you learned that selling sex or performing sexy was a way to make money? How did you find out, and what was your immediate reaction?

The first time I really learned about sex work was when I first saw the film *Pretty Woman*, and I was around thirteen. I knew I wasn't allowed to be watching the film, but it made an impression on me because it was sexy and I felt connected to the main character. It was a story of following your dreams and signs, leading you to a different life, and that was impactful to me as a child. I thought of her as empowered and free and wanted to be like her. I may have known about sex workers vaguely before that, but they were just negative connotations in my mind.

Did you know it would be something that you would do for income at that point?

I felt like it could be a viable option for my future.

When did you decide to trade sex/ualized services?

It was in 2012, when my partner and I founded Beyondeep Productions and created our first porn for a film festival!

Did you start out in a line of sex work you thought you would want to continue in, or were you treading water and learning with a plan to change it up? Club jumping counts here. Can you talk about why?
When we created our first porn, "Beyondeep," we submitted it to a porn film festival in hopes of winning a cash prize. We did not know that being in this festival would spark us to continue making porn and doing other types of sex work! When the festival decided to censor and edit out some explicit content from our film, we knew this content was vital to keep putting out there. Creating more visibility for Black queer and trans people has been our goal ever since.

What are some songs that were popular or that you loved when you first started doing sex work?
When I first started doing sex work, I loved listening to songs by Gangsta Boo, like "Where Dem Dollas At" and "Can I Get Paid." Also, Rihanna's "Pour It Up," Spice's "So Mi Like It," and "Freak Like Me" by Adina Howard are some of my faves. Still listen to them now, but I have to add Megan Thee Stallion, who always gets me pumped—love her song "Sugar Baby."

What do you do to relax after a bad shift or client?
To relax, I like to smoke a thick joint and light some candles on my altar, try to transform the energy with some cleansing herbs or essential oils! Wash myself down with some herbal soap.

Do you feel like having done sex work has given you certain skills that are useful in your day-to-day or non-swing life that others don't have? What are some of them? Are there disadvantages from sex work that also come up? If there are, will you elaborate on them?
I've always been a sexual healer since before it was my trade, and I feel like this healing power is useful in my partnerships and also in understanding how to transform energy and read other people's energy in a way that some people may not be as open to or aware of. Being open to explore my sexuality and feel empowered in it has helped me be a more open person overall. Learning and being a part of people's varying desires and fantasies through sex work helps me understand people better in general.

The only disadvantage to doing sex work for me has been having to deal with all the negative stigma I face being open and public as a sex worker. People have negative connotations about sex workers because there aren't many empowering portrayals of sex workers, and I think that living my life and being close to other sex workers has made me a more open, understanding, and empathic person.

What do you think would make sex workers' lives better or easier or safer (or all three)?

Sex workers' lives would be better if there were more accessible housing and holistic health care, if sex work were decriminalized, if there were more empowering depictions of sex work/ers in the media, if rapists and abusers were actually held accountable, and if there were a true end to rape culture.

Do you feel like you're a part of a larger community of sex workers? In person or on the Internet?

I do feel like I'm part of a larger community of sex workers! Not so much in person right now, but through the Internet. There are so many amazing Black queer and trans sex workers that I have linked up with through social media. And so many dope virtual erotic events that I would not know about if I was not online.

How do you see power dynamics play out in your community? What kind of workers are valued by other sex workers around you, and what kind of work is most valued?

I see power dynamics play out in the adult film industry through people continuing to prioritize white and heteronormative views. Indie companies and Black queer trans performers are sidelined and disrespected, constantly receiving less for their labor or placed in disempowered or exoticized positions. It supports rape culture and is typically catering toward a "male fantasy." As more visibility has been possible through the Internet, there is a growing niche for "ethical porn" that supports Black queer trans sex work and more "realistic" portrayals of sexuality.

Regardless of whether you're involved in activism or organizing, what do you see as important goals for us to work toward?

Important goals for us to work toward are the empowerment and inclusion of Black trans and queer people in everything we do. Showing love toward Black trans and queer people by getting us jobs, resources, features, and paying us well for our labor.

What do you think are barriers to achieving those goals?
The only barrier to achieving these goals is our egos. We need to see past the barriers of our different identities and internalized judgments and be more willing to give in order to receive. If we exist in true spaces of love, it is easy to spread love to others!

How are you coping with our current reality?
Currently because of COVID, I am doing a lot of virtual work. And you can find us on Instagram and Twitter at @beyondeep.

What would you like to see from white sex workers moving forward? Individually and/or as a community and/or as organizers?
I would like to see more white sex workers featuring and promoting Black sex workers on their platforms! And showing more love to Black people in general. Speaking on the inequality within the industry and actually advocating for Black and nonwhite sex workers to be paid more.

Where do you hope to be in five years? Don't let the current state of reality hold you back: what's your ideal world that you want to be living in in five years?
In five years, I will be living my life to the fullest, with good health, wealth, peace, and love. Ideally homelessness would no longer be, weed and sex work would be legal and fully decriminalized, we would have universal health care, and Black trans people would be able to live safe and prosper in all the ways.

El Cerrito

Nick Lovett

One of my most memorable clients was a man who owned a mansion in the El Cerrito hills.

We met at a Peet's Coffee in Berkeley. I had gone shopping for my outfit the day prior, picking out a black dress with big white flowers plastered over it. I still have it hanging in my closet—glancing at it always beckons a chill to run over my body.

Upon meeting, he told me that he was nervous; he'd never done this before. I laughed and reassured him that it would be fine, even though I had never done this before either. What did being a sugar baby even mean? Was I really endangering my life, as the sites I'd read for advice had cautioned?

I tired of his company quickly. He wanted me to genuinely love him, which I just couldn't bring myself to do. We kissed in his truck before we invaded the public for our dates. It must have been a sight to see an old, athletic white man with a young, fat Black girl. Unfortunately, no one ever said anything. In El Cerrito, he would pick me up from the BART station and drop me back off after he was done fucking me. His mansion had a grand, elaborately designed gate, and we were tucked up in his room, far from the neighbors. I sometimes wondered, if I screamed, would anyone hear me?

"I love you" he said, handing over a grand in cash
I gazed longingly at the green exhibition, in awe of its beauty I found my response.
"I love you too"
By Elizabeth Juarez

During one of our sessions, he was hovering over my bare body, preparing to enter me. I stopped him for a request.

"Can you turn the lights off?" I asked. I was self-conscious, but more than that, I didn't want to see his white, wrinkled body in such detail.

"What, why?" he shot back. My response wasn't good enough, I suppose, and we had sex with the lights on. I pretended to cum as he came, and then slowly gathered my things from one corner of his house to the other. Cash money in my hand, I began opting to take Uber back to El Cerrito's BART station after our sessions. Swooping down the winding streets, my vagina throbbing between my legs in pain and my head in a blank daze, I started to wonder what the fuck I was doing.

Of course, I felt like the relationship was beneficial for me financially. I was able to buy textbooks I needed, buy drugs to numb the pain from being alive, and engage in fun, mindless activities like taking Uber wherever the fuck I wanted without having to be concerned about the cost. But he couldn't meet as frequently as I would have liked, flaked on paying me as much as we agreed, and seemed increasingly entitled to my time.

He could tell as I grew tired of him. During our last meeting, in which he forced himself in my mouth, I gagged and thought of death. I attempted to leave earlier than we had agreed. "See, it's time, so-and-so," I said casually as I dried myself down from our shower and collected my things.

He proceeded to make a fuss, lecturing me and putting me down. I eyed the door, him between me and the exit. I wondered if I would make it out alive.

I did.

There are details omitted from this story that are only for me and my heart. But I still remember the blinding sunset we could see from his achingly tall windows, the lush of green that I would look out at while in the shower sucking his cock, and the exquisite taste of the wine I'll never be able to afford that he poured for me.

But most of all, I remember the fear. The fear when it felt like his cock would drop into my throat, when it felt like my uterus would shatter from his force, his front door that looked on, beckoning me to leave, quick.

And as I left, he laughed, and when I got home, I cried.

Art by Eva Wǒ

6 gifts you can ask your sugar daddy for that won't destroy his sense of your "quirk" as unthreatening sexual garnish and that won't make you feel like you have turned into a cartoon glyph with tits animated by the dispossessed spirit of capitalist alienation

Cisqo Thyme

SunnyLife Metal Straws, $16.00, Color: Rose Gold
He thinks: You care about the environment! Look at you sipping a calorie-free Starbucks beverage out of one of these, look at your *lips* on this *straw, puckered, sucking,* caring *so much* about the oceans ...
For real: You are a capable bitch with a diverse group of friends and I guarantee somehow you can get use of literally thirty seconds at a machine shop. Cut each of these babies in thirds or quarters and *bang,* your cold-copped taco powder is luxxx.

Stella Corkscrew and Bottle Opener, $42.00, Color: White
He thinks: Look at the polka dots! Look how cute! It's like his daughter's bedroom sheets, the daughter you have so much in common with; the one who he wishes you could meet, 'cause maybe you could explain that he's not so bad; the one who used to have hair like yours before she cut it all off because of that liberal college her mother let her go to; the one who was so happy in high school when she and her nice pretty friends would hang out in the kitchen all afternoon in their soccer shorts and little sports bras—that one!
For real: Best case, this removes the packaging that stands in the way of your Trader Joe's anesthesia. Worst case: twenty-five to life.

Pretty Useful Tools Manicure Kit, $49.00, Color: Multi

He thinks: For those evenings you're apart from him that you spend at home, lounging around in lingerie, writhing on the bed, masturbating with the dildo that reminds you of him, thinking of his big, strong grown-man cock and the way it makes you come over and over again by banging in and out of you very, very fast, calling his name. In between flicking the bean, teehee, you can use this manicure set on your feminine hands, making those nails pink and clean and perfect for gently raking through the buzz-clipped hair on his neck wrinkles while you whisper how wet you are.

For real: For obsessive/self-harm tweezing and picking, obviously, and if no one has a grinder.

KOOLTAIL Plaid Dog Hoodie Pet Clothes Sweaters with Hat, $17.99

You love your pets and you characterize them how you prefer, and when they beg for food you say they're greedy and they love you. You think they think cute things, mostly about you, and then you tell them they are thinking those things and they stare at you. You use them for emotional support and are annoyed when they have personality traits that aren't what you would like. You think they are totally different than other creatures who are not that different from them, other creatures who are part of cruel and depersonalizing systems, the fruits of which you enjoy! So this Xmas you and your sugar daddy can agree that he should get you this adorable dog sweater.

Pendleton Women's Cable Gloves, $35.99

He thinks: He's keeping his baby warm, and these are pink, and pretty girls love pink, and they aren't that expensive!

For real: You don't have *daddy issues* so much as you have *alienated from your family, constantly uncovering new ways that a childhood of benign neglect continues to manifest in all of your unconscious behavior issues,* which is a pretty annoying jump scare to have on the daily. You would never buy gloves for yourself, because they aren't a necessity, obviously, but if someone gives them to you, it's nice to not have frozen hands. You can be grateful toward He Who Gave Them to You and perhaps temporarily exist in a sicksweet fog of affection and protection. Maybe you can Velveteen Rabbit the fake feelings into reality? At least it will be easier to perform "cheerful and in love" for an evening, though the pressure drop when he shoves his furred tongue down your throat and says he respects you so much and that's why you're his favorite slut will be epic. That's okay! The trauma will make you more compassionate, and you still have these gloves: when he insists you take his wrinkly hand in public to show all passersby that he's fucking you, you won't have to touch his skin.

Kiki De Montparnasse Women's Icon Lace Balconette Bra, $295
Kiki De Montparnasse Women's Icon Lace High-Waist Shorts, $275
The combined price of these items is a staggering $570, and you can get something that looks almost exactly like it on Yandy for $25, or at least similar enough for a thirsty tennis coach with a Viagra prescription. Tell him you want this but you aren't sure of the sizing because something-something breasts/ass/whatever, and then return it for an Amazon credit of $550, which you can use on things that aren't tiny useless pieces of lace, like food or laundry detergent. You still can't use it on rent—when I figure out how to convert lingerie to rent, I will blast that knowledge to the heavens.

Club, by Manon

I Don't Consent to Enthusiastic Consent

Phoenix Calida

I have a request for feminists, leftists, and anyone who may otherwise be considered a dreaded social justice warrior.

No, *request* isn't the right word, because this is actually a demand. And it's a big one. Ready? Here goes:

Stop telling me how to fuck.

The first instinct many have is to pull back and get defensive: "I am a feminist/leftist/progressive. I don't control women's bodies or tell them how to fuck. I am not a conservative!"

And yet, I am constantly being told how to fuck, when to fuck, who I can fuck, and whether or not my consent was valid. By self-proclaimed fellow leftists.

How is this possible in the allegedly sexually liberated circles of the left?

Because I've done sex work. And too often, enthusiastic consent culture and sex workers' rights don't mix.

What began as a way to empower women, shift narratives around consent, and challenge conservative ideas around sexuality has become a weapon used to belittle, shame, and outright deny lived experiences of certain women, mainly sex workers and those who fall outside of white, cis, heterosexual norms.

Granted, consent is a complicated topic. Consent requires nuance. But consent, particularly enthusiastic consent, is often oversimplified and, as a result, leaves large swaths of the population out of the discussion.

While I certainly understand the purpose of teaching enthusiastic consent, it has ultimately barred people like me from being able to participate in conversations around what idealistic consent versus realistic consent looks like.

A few years ago, it seemed only a handful of lefty feminist-leaning outlets talked about enthusiastic consent. However, in a post-#MeToo era, the topic of enthusiastic consent has not only come back but is more popular than ever in the mainstream—and I've never been more excluded.

Enthusiastic consent was meant to modernize and revolutionize the slogan "no means no." It is true, "no means no" is antiquated and lacks nuance. There are several reasons that "no means no" fails us. Some people don't want to say yes, but are scared to say no. Due to trauma, some people freeze up and remain silent instead of saying no. Some outdated laws still suggest that rape isn't really rape if the victim is passed out and unable to say no. For example, there was the NYC district attorney who warned that severely intoxicated women aren't technically covered under the state's rape laws,[1] as well as the terrifying real-life case in which an Oklahoma court ruled that forced oral sex isn't rape if the victim had passed out from drinking.[2]

There is also the now-infamous Rick Ross line in the song "U.O.E.N.O.":

> Put molly in her champagne, she ain't even know it
> I took her home, I enjoyed that, she ain't even know it

These lyrics resulted in the mocking of women across social media for being too sensitive over a joke—as if rape jokes that mirror real life are funny.

Enthusiastic consent sought to save us from those forms of rape culture. Enthusiastic consent, according to an ironically named website called Respect Yourself, tells us:

> To make things a bit clearer we like to talk about enthusiastic
> consent. That way there is no confusion. Enthusiastic consent
> works on the premise that both partners should be engaging in

any sort of sexual activity with gusto—with enthusiasm. So when you are kissing your partner, they are kissing you back (sticking their tongue down your throat!). When you are pulling your top off, they are ripping theirs off ... if they aren't engaging, then assume they are not ready.[3]

Or, as Jessica Valenti and Jaclyn Freidman put it: "The 'yes means yes' philosophy is that the only valid sexual consent is enthusiastic consent."[4]

This sounds lovely ... and unrealistic. I am certain it's helpful to those in new relationships, or to those experiencing sexual relationships for the first time, or to those just beginning to consider what their own personal consent looks like. This definition, however, doesn't work for a lot of other folks, namely sex workers. Many sex workers give consent, but they don't always do it enthusiastically. Instead of discussing the nuance of consent, many with anti-sex work stances have instead begun suggesting that all sex work is rape and that sex workers cannot truly consent because money has changed hands, or because money was what created consent in the first place.

I'm often told on social media that every sex work interaction I engaged in was rape because I didn't "enthusiastically" consent. I am told that because I wouldn't have had sex with certain clients without money, my consent doesn't count. I am told that I am not having sex properly and I need to be saved from myself. Oddly enough, I am told this most often by saviors who don't consent to respecting my boundaries or space. I have been called vile names, and when I ask for that verbal abuse to stop, or when I ask to be referred to as a sex worker instead of a "prostituted woman," those boundaries are never met with consent. It's ironic that in order to "save me," my saviors must degrade me, violate my boundaries, and then still lecture me about how I am too ignorant to understand what consent truly is.

The anti-sex work movement wants me to view myself as nothing more than a perpetual victim without agency. Their goal is to end demand and save me from myself, no matter the cost.

Is it any wonder, then, that the same white, middle-class, predominantly cis and heterosexual women who gave us enthusiastic consent as the *exclusive* model of consent are also the same ones who use government crackdowns, police brutality, loss of civil liberties, and social stigma to save sex workers from themselves?

This generation has a new set of liberal saviors, but the cost is still lethal to the sex work community. We're moving away from more conservative views around sex work and the idea that sex workers are just immoral and lazy, but we're moving toward a framework that paints every sex worker as nothing more than a hurt puppy dog in need of rescue.

In attempting to liberate sex workers, and instead of actually listening to what we need, those trying to save us have created a new obstacle in our fight for rights and dignity. The sex work community, especially the nonwhite sex work community, finds itself in a very precarious position. Where we used to be victims of bad policies intended to punish sex workers, now we are victims of bad policies created to rescue sex workers. Sadly, under both models, sex workers are seen as inferior, incapable, and undeserving of autonomy. We've gone from the idea that sex workers don't deserve autonomy because we are villains, and villains don't deserve nice things, to the idea that sex workers don't deserve autonomy because we are too stupid to know how to appreciate it.

Where do I turn to be free? Where do I go to have my own experiences validated, understood, and accepted? Where do I go to reclaim my own sexual experiences? Not to the enthusiastic consent community, it seems.

The irony is thick here. Historically, under the idea that sex workers should be vilified, Black women are seen as hypersexual deviants, unable to be raped because we were too full of lust to be able to say no to any man. Now, as a Black sex worker, under models that victimize sex workers, I cannot be anything other than a rape victim, because white feminism has dictated that I am not capable of saying yes. Either way, I have no autonomy in the eyes of lawmakers and policy pushers. The cost of this arrogance has been fatal to my community.

Where does this leave me? Where does this leave my trauma? Where does this leave the sex work community? Under enthusiastic consent, there is no nuance. I am told there is no useful distinction between discussing an instance of nonenthusiastic consent and flat-out rape because—in theory—these experiences are the same. I didn't give enthusiastic consent when I was paid. I didn't give any consent when I was raped. But as long as all consent *must* be enthusiastic, neither of these scenarios are deemed truly consensual.

I have done sex work for quite some time, sometimes even street based. I can assure any inquiring mind that getting paid to do something

I wasn't really into was nothing like being held down and raped against my will.

And yet I am not allowed to discuss this distinction, because the only qualifier to fucking is, "But were you into it?"

What if I wasn't and my consent was still valid?

There is something beyond simple arrogance in telling someone you have a right to dictate their autonomy and their consent. Suddenly, despite being surrounded by liberals and feminists, I am still denied the agency I desire. I am still not allowed to truly live or experience a full range of humanity and human sexual experience, because I am a victim who doesn't understand how sex works.

This is terrifyingly similar to old arguments about sex workers: we weren't allowed to be full, multifaceted humans, because only "bad" women would go into sex work in the first place.

Under each mindset, I am reduced to a thing. I am either seen as an evil thing to be loathed and disgusted by my superiors or as a broken, incompetent thing that must be saved by my superiors.

In reality, I am neither. I am a person with autonomy, trying to make my way in this world. What I need is for stigma to end, for people to treat me with dignity and respect. I need nuance around the topic of consent.

I need to be heard. I have a voice, and it works just fine ... unless you don't want to hear it.

Not everyone fucks enthusiastically. And that's perfectly okay. I don't always fuck enthusiastically. That doesn't mean my yes wasn't a real yes. My no is no, my yes is yes, and this is not up for debate or outside interpretation.

My consent counts even if it doesn't meet an arbitrary standard set by liberal feminists.

Stop telling sex workers what our consent looks like. We have a right to consent on our own terms. Learn to embrace that.

Learn to embrace us.

Learn to respect us.

Learn to give us dignity.

Enthusiastically.

Notes

1   Chris Glorioso and Evan Stulberger, "I-Team: Manhattan District Attorney Says New York Rape Law Fails to Protect Drunk Women," *NBC New York*, August 29,

2019, https://www.nbcnewyork.com/news/local/date-rape-alcohol-drinking-women-manhattan-district-attorney-cy-vance-investigation/1049170.

2   Molly Redden, "Oklahoma Court: Oral Sex Is Not Rape If Victim Is Unconscious from Drinking," *Guardian*, April 27, 2016, https://www.theguardian.com/society/2016/apr/27/oral-sex-rape-ruling-tulsa-oklahoma-alcohol-consent.

3   "Enthusiastic Consent," Respect Yourself, accessed September 22, 2022, https://respectyourself.info/sex/consent/enthusiastic-consent.

4   Jaclyn Friedman and Jessica Valenti, eds., *Yes Means Yes!: Visions of Female Sexual Power & a World without Rape* (Berkeley, CA: Seal Press, 2008).

When My Mom Found My Craigslist Ad

Alyssa Pariah

January 2005. Central NJ erotic services. "t4m - fresh vers shemale - 18"

She kicked me out of our apartment my senior year. I had already given up on school anyway and she saw it. All I cared about was transitioning. To be able to look in the mirror in peace. Maybe catch a sugar daddy and get the fuck out of New Jersey.[1]

She printed it out just like they do at hotels when they make you leave and threaten to call the cops on you. She pushed it in my face, wanting a response. I couldn't. My throat had collapsed and dropped into my stomach already. She's the most confrontational woman on Earth. My peripheral vision got blurry until I blacked out totally.

I don't remember how I managed to get words out, but I took the paper out of her hands and said I'm sorry for being such a disappointment. I had secretly known for some time that I was certainly not going to go to college or start a career or a family. Those were options only if I could manage to trick myself out of being trans. But when I became suicidal enough, I knew it was Delestrogen or jumping off the George Washington Bridge.

She cursed me out, saying out loud the nagging thoughts in my head:

You're wasting your talents!

You used to be so smart!

What happened to dreaming of being a child psychologist?

What if you get killed, raped, infected?

You're lazy.

You're selfish.

Get out. I don't want you anymore.

I stayed at my grandmother's house and did actually manage to grad-uate high school. But it was only because I used to let an administrator blow me sometimes so he'd smudge my disciplinary and attendance records. I continued to hoe.

The story I kept telling myself was that because my mom had been strung out on heroin, I'd had to raise myself. She was not in a position to cast me away for something like this. Her most recent attempt to get clean seemed to be working. She was doing the methadone program and was enrolled in night school. She made amends to me per her twelve-step program for all the horrendous shit that I had to learn in order to survive her neglect. I forgave her and I fucking meant it. How could she not extend me my grace back?

Since kindergarten, I covered up that she wasn't home most of the time. That we ran away from my father because he repeatedly nearly killed us. That she was on dope and he was on crack. I had to be convinc-ing to keep the social workers away so we could keep our housing and benefits. So I wouldn't be taken away to foster care, and her to prison. My biggest fears I obsessed over. So no, I wasn't open to her judgment and punishment after all of that.

It was some sniveling piece of shit in her Narcotics Anonymous home group that sent her the link to my ad. It humiliated her. But she was no stranger to selling it her damn self. She had done all types of dirt in her day to get money. I knew about it all. But throwing it, or anything else, in her face at that point seemed like a cheap shot that might make her relapse. So I always kept it to myself. To protect her pride. Every time I heard someone in the family talk shit about her parenting, call her a junkie, or whatever the fuck, I shut them out. I became the irritating, opinionated little faggot they'd accused me of being. My God, was I a resentful child!

They wanted me to spend time with my father on weekends to learn how to be a man. I was appalled by this. Didn't they see his rage at me? Did they not remember my battered mother in the hospital? My father had made it plain to me that I was just like my mother. The way I rolled my eyes and sucked my teeth and rested my hands on my hips. I had internalized that deeply. We hated each other. We still do.

You see, this is the nitty-gritty shit that doesn't fit so nicely in the narratives of trans childhood. My mother says she always knew but didn't say anything because she was nervous and humiliated about it. This is learned behavior, so I became nervous and humiliated too. Of course, my classmates were put off by me. I had seething contempt for the little shitheads and was always on edge, ready for some oncoming attack or insult. I couldn't discuss this with her when I got home, though, because I knew it would trigger her. I knew she couldn't hold my stuff on top of her own. Year after year, she watched me retreat and give up emotionally. She wanted to intervene, but dope came first.

All this is the stuff of preparation for prostitution at a young age. Sex, gender, money: these three are tangled in knots that I haven't even tried to unravel yet.[2] I learned about fetishism for shemales when I got the Internet, and I sold my cock and ass for money so I could pay for feminization. But this is a serious trauma that I didn't consider would cause a lasting stress disorder. My mother implored me to wait to transition. Until after college and a career maybe. She told me horror stories of trans women she knew from the streets who were found murdered and mutilated. If she had to bury me, she told me she wouldn't forgive me.

She screamed and cried about it. But I retorted that the idea of letting puberty finish the job was simply worse than death. Period.

Lying, I told her I would try to wait. I didn't. I met older femqueens in the Village, cutting school. This is so typical for queer youth that it exhausts me to have to tell this part of my story. *Yes!* Parents regularly reject their own children when they come out or are outed. Often, their classmates at school bully them, and they go to gay neighborhoods in nearby cities to try to find love. Sometimes they do find love. But they usually find danger too: predatory adults who have a taste for young sad gurlz.

I met men on the street who said things to me that confused me. It was disorienting to get complimented for precisely what had been a source of derision. I was afraid of them but also turned on. I didn't get to have puppy love or high school dating. I was treated as a hated fag who now had the audacity to start calling himself a girl. What a joke! Despite my compulsion to feminize myself, I didn't actually think I was beautiful.

I didn't have self-esteem. But I'm pretty sure that's part of the allure for these men who come on to people like us.

The older femqueens I got close to gave it to me straight. Yes, these tranny-chasing pedos are dangerous, but they pay. You just have to work them, and they showed me how to do it. I lost my virginity on East 94th Street in some guy's bathroom. I don't know who else was in the apartment, but that's why we were in there. He didn't explain much. It didn't seem like a big deal to him. So I went with it. It was over in a few minutes and I got two hundred dollars. I did two other tricks that night. Six hundred dollars.

I bought hormones and some stuff from the beauty supply store. The rest of the money I gave to a laser hair-removal technician in Alphabet City. My five-o'clock shadow had to go. I was disgusted with myself to the core, but smooth skin would assuage that. Right?

When I went back to school the following Monday, some of my insecurity seemed to have dissipated, like I was slightly above what had made me feel buried the Friday before my first weekend of whoring. It wasn't that I had a positive outlook now, but there was something else on my mind other than the familiar alienation. A sick distraction.

When I got home, instead of doing any homework, I was corresponding by email with men who were excited to be in touch with me. I understood that this wasn't care or love or anything good, really. But it was exhilarating. I was investing in my transition. Planning an escape from my pathetic life once I was an adult. I did it every day after school. Many days instead of school.

My mother started noticing physical changes, but she didn't press me about anything at first. Not until she saw the gruesome proof on Craigslist with her own eyes. I could tell she had become tired of being worried about me. She was focused on getting her life together. I wasn't even mad about it. Hopefully, I would soon be able to protect myself so she wouldn't have to bury me. That's still my main motivator now.[3]

Bettie's Responses

1   How many of us started hoeing on Craigslist? The erotic services section helped me pay for my education. It feels almost quaint to think about now, but that was an entire other world.

2   "All this is the stuff of preparation for prostitution at a young age. Sex, gender, money" is so succinct, and so real. If these three intersections don't line up in very specific ways, your chances of doing sex work are much higher. For better

or worse. Racialized and gendered bodies, especially those considered abject in some way, are more likely to have some connection to sex work.

3   When I was working the most, a keen understanding that I did not want my mama to bury me kept me focused on safety. Knowing that I needed to make sure my decisions didn't hurt her was extremely important to me.

Art by Kat Salas

Crystal Kimewon

Editor's Note: This is condensed and lightly edited from a phone interview I did with Crystal in February of 2021.

I've heard a lot of people say, you know, that "[missing and murdered Indigenous women wouldn't be dead] if they weren't in sex work, if they didn't choose sex work," like it's a choice. More or less blaming their lifestyle for being murdered. If I can shine light in that area ... we don't choose this.

We look at the overrepresentation of Indigenous children within the foster care system, the child welfare system everywhere, not only Canada.

This is just my story. That's the only thing I can speak to.

In my teen years, I was classified as a hard-to-serve, high-risk, high-needs child. Early-onset depression, you know, posttraumatic stress, [from] my own personal life as a child living with my mother who was an alcoholic and who was herself a product of the child welfare system. I struggled with addiction. There was domestic violence, the end being my mom had been charged with manslaughter. She had killed my brother's father—we had separate fathers—in the home while we were there. That was the start of Crown wardship. So, Crown wardship: my legal guardian was the child welfare system.

As a teenager, they put the more difficult kids within the group home system—that's a private system. Privately owned group homes and whatnot. There are ministry standards, but they're privately owned; like Northern Lights owns, I think, four group homes in our city. Canada's different in that way.

We have Native child welfare now, where a lot of First Nations communities are taking control of child welfare; however, we're still governed by these Western child welfare guidelines and policies.

When we took all our kids back, under this legislation that says we can have custody of our Indigenous children finally, we didn't have enough trained supervisors or managers to be able to handle the influx of children we were taking back from mainstream child welfare. So many workers lost their jobs because all the kids that were in the mainstream system are now under the control of First Nations and communities. Where do our managers and supervisors come from? From the main-stream child welfare. They took the jobs within the Native orgs. A lot of them are white; a lot of them, we call them apples. You're red on the outside, but on the inside, you function like a white person.

To me, how I look at it now, it's our own people who are inflicting harm on our family system, but that's a whole other issue.

Transferring from the foster system to the group home system—the group homes are in urban areas. I was this little rural Indian living with white people primarily through my childhood, and then I transitioned into these group home systems, where there's a lot of other troubled girls. I met a lot of girls and other foster children in my younger years, and we looked out for each other within the system. There was an older teenage girl, a Native girl, from a nearby reserve; you kind of take one another under your wing. I was always sad to see them go: the abuse would start again as soon as someone who had been watching over my brother and I had left the foster home. A lot of girls from the rez, they're tough girls; they're not afraid to say what's on their mind, whatever it may be. You have that strong protective factor, because a lot of us grow up raising our younger siblings through our parents' addiction, so that nurturing, that constant looking out for each other, it's there when it comes to that traumatic childhood.

In the group home system, you're left with all the trauma of passing through that system and all the hurts, all the ugly that comes with it. So naturally, a coping mechanism, or whatever you want to call it, is drugs.

My drug of choice was opiates and heroin. I didn't want to be an alcoholic, because my mother was one, so I justified my use by, "At least I'm not a drunk like my mom."

I was reasonably good at stealing, but I was also getting heavily into drugs, which brought me closer to other girls that were within the system and involved in sex work. It was more connection, connection on the street level, as a foster child that was constantly running away from the group home.

I was tired of this system that, in my eyes, didn't fucking protect me. Life was worse; it would have been better with my mom. I was running from this system that never heard us when we cried out, never believed us when we said that abuse was happening, that abuse was in the home. My mother actually got shot, and child welfare, psychiatrists, lawyers had this story where my mother ended up getting charged and she went to jail for it.

We're living with all of that, right? I hate the system. I'm a social worker now, but I could never work with child welfare, just because it's the same policies.

On the streets, there were a lot of people from our culture. We knew each other's stories; trauma connected us. We didn't know it then. She was no better than me, I was no better than her, our backgrounds were the same, so there was that connection.

You had sex workers walking the street in Sudbury that were dressed up. They looked nice, they got out of a car, whoever their pimp was, was taking care of them. Or maybe it was their boyfriend, I don't know. That interaction between Indigenous sex workers and white sex workers twenty years ago—it wasn't like it is now. I'm in Toronto now, and our girls, it's a family; it's very diverse here in Toronto, obviously, versus in Sudbury. Up north, you still see a lot of racism, discrimination, stuff like that. A lot of the pimps were white. Sudbury was not as diverse as an urban area, like Toronto is. So it was really … they had a place to stay, it wasn't a nice place. It was usually like a trap-house-type setting; the street girls stayed there, a guy might have paid the rent and fed them drugs, nice clothes.

There's a huge gap in service delivery catering to the needs of Indigenous sex workers. I was involved in Sex Workers Advisory Network in the northern region, and it was very pro-sex work, very "How can we support you in this?" But there was never a door. There was never an escape door, there was never a way out, and why aren't they offering a way out? I understand we should be supportive if they choose to be in this lifestyle, but a lot of our Indigenous girls are here because of addiction. You can tell they don't take pride in their work; they're not proud of what they're doing.

So there's the idea, "We choose this lifestyle and therefore are deserving of the consequences that happen when we're on the streets and doing this type of work," and the way white men and society views the Indigenous woman, with that discrimination and racist. It's a tough life—it's a tough lifestyle or career choice or whatever you want to call it—to get out of. And if those supports aren't there?

I know a lot of Indigenous orgs are anti-human trafficking, they're taking that spin on it. I don't know if it's because that's where the funding comes from, but if you go to a Native org and they have a worker specific to anti-human trafficking, a lot of that is tied into Missing and Murdered Indigenous Women. The funding we get is because there's a shit pool of funding for women who are being murdered.

We're pulling it from that reality; it's sad in that way. I've been within non-Indigenous, primarily white, pro-sex work services, agencies, and I don't know if they can't grasp it or if they refuse to or if they've just got fucking blinders on.

It was tough because you're constantly—we have this idea as Indigenous helpers, we have this two-eyed seeing, it's called, where we're looking at the reality of it, which is the Indigenous worldview: understanding all that trauma and abuse our people have gone through, and working that approach, but we're also understanding that a lot of the money that we get is governed by Western policies, seeing a need and that goal we're to meet. You're constantly shifting and adapting how you deliver services based on what your ministry guidelines are for that funding. So, having workers at street level that are willing to go and step outside that box, willing to go the extra mile, willing to go beyond what is simply required of them: let's hand out condoms, let's give the girls sandwiches, let's encourage them, and all that sort of stuff. Let's ask those questions that our policy isn't requiring us to ask but we know that no one is asking these girls.

This goes for non-Indigenous girls as well, but there are no services tailored to meeting the needs of the Indigenous sex worker. The

Indigenous sex worker is murdered or goes missing, because of how society views her within that lifestyle, a lifestyle that a lot of us don't choose. It's a means to an end. It's often chosen because we need to keep getting that drug or we're going to get sick or ...

The instance I shared with you about being on the streets with the Indigenous girl I was in foster care with and watching her get beat, and watching white people, people coming from the YMCA with children, adults, couples, coming from bars, walking past and seeing a white man beat an Indigenous woman in an alley, and nobody coming to help–that really reinforced what I already knew, what I was feeling. Everything that I had gone through in foster care, we tried to speak the truth; we tried to reach out for help, but nobody helped us.

All we really had was each other on the street. We had to look out for each other.

A lot of these girls still worked for white pimps–they had better drugs or whatever–but there were Indigenous men on the street, they were often homeless or often transient, passing from city to city to city, and they would have multiple girlfriends. They would never take money, but they would make sure that when she showed up with a swollen eye from her white pimp, that he took care of her.

This Indigenous man–I was seeing him, he was seeing two other girls, they were swers on the street. There was that sense of community, that communal factor we have within a lot of Indigenous societies from time prior contact. And he made sure there was food, a warm place, a safer place to stay. It was short lived–they'd travel to the next city–but there were safe places on the street that were open to multiple girls. And it wasn't like the relationships the girls had with the white pimps: you felt like he cared, like he was looking out. But at the same time, [abuse] was still happening, but there was that sense of comfort, there was that sense of "It's going to be okay. You're going to get out of this."

I lived–it's no longer up, it burned down, but one of our more well-known trap houses back in the day, it was a rooming house, and I shared it with this man, and shared time. It was almost like a communal ... what do you call it, those polygamists? I was watching that show and was like, *Oh, that's kind of like how we lived when we were teenagers.* And you just shared, because you knew you'd be taken care of.

There was a sense of looking out for one another. I don't think I ever met, even as a social worker, an Indigenous sex worker who was so fucking pro about it the way I look at a white activist or sex worker, who is very "We have a right to choose" and, you know, reclaiming the word *whore* and all this stuff with fierce fuckin' ownership and whatnot. You don't see a lot of Indigenous women on the front lines.

I can only speak from my experience and perspective and what I've noticed, and I always go back to, a lot of our women, when you look at an Indigenous person as a whole, as a whole being, there is a physical component, there's a mental component, there's a spiritual component, and there's an emotional component. Every person has them. When you look at the well-being—you ever see those really old tops? You press the top and they spin? Ideally, when we're ideally balanced, we're like that, spinning, perfectly in sync, level.

Now when you look at the emotional aspect of a person and the trauma that they have gone through, be it incest, sexual assault, all these results of the residential school system, the past system imposed on First Nations people, indigenous people—there's a whole generation after generation of trauma. You could say that trauma goes even deeper; it's a blood memory. We're born with trauma and we don't even ... we can have a healthy upbringing, we can have a mom and dad that are together, but that trauma is in our DNA, it's in our blood memory.

So when you look at the whole person, emotionally, she's scarred from this stuff.

Mentally, maybe she didn't finish school. Maybe the mother's alcoholism impacted her ability to comprehend certain things and how society works and views her. You see that often. Or you see a lot of just grade eight, nine education with a lot of our people.

We're generally a very minimalist people. It doesn't take a lot, we don't thrive on the luxury of white society. It's really more the simple things that give us peace in our being.

And peace in my being, when I was on the street, was having that sense of family, street respect. When you look at the Indigenous woman and the intergenerational effects of what she's gone through, and her mother before her and her grandmother before her, her ability to speak up—how many times have I tried to speak up? And nobody fucking listened. How many times have I tried to scream out and nobody turned their head or came to the rescue?

Standing on the front lines of this cause, "pro-sex work," when so many [Indigenous women] are treated with far more disrespect, far more discrimination [than white women]—the acts of racism and beatings, you hear so many different stories of Indigenous women who were sex workers who died in hotels, and these men, they get little to no time.

How I view it? Pro-sex work is an important front to be standing on if you're in a well and balanced place and have reclaimed so much of who you are, as an Indigenous woman, and you've found your confidence and your voice to stand and advocate for those women who are on the street.

But then you're also standing alongside so many other white women who fiercely reclaimed their voice but have no comprehension of the [reality of] Indigenous women on the street. So not only are you fighting for the woman on the street, you're also educating everybody standing on the front line with you, and that is fucking exhausting.

I lean on allies so much, people who are woke to the issues our people are facing, when I'm tired. We need that—as Indigenous advocates and people on the front lines, we need that support. We don't need to be influenced; we need you to be able to listen, we need to tell you what it is we need. Give her a voice, don't impose your ideals and perspective on her. Give her a voice, no one's ever said to her, "Your voice matters." We're imposing this ideal—when you talk about pro-sex work—this understanding, on Indigenous sex workers. That's my view. I've always struggled with that in working alongside white women. I'm very for a woman's right to choose. If she wants to do sex work, I'm there. Tell me what you need. But at the same time, through all of that, I saw so many gaps in service provision for the Indigenous street worker.

And not everyone's story is going to be like mine. But a lot of ours . . . that's the reality of it.

I'm in the Toronto region. I know we have Maggie's; we have a version of SWAN down here. In our northern communities, it's difficult. We're still unlearning a lot of shit; we're still having to do a lot of education with non-Indigenous agencies. You come to a more rural area—I don't know how it is in the States, but Toronto's fairly multicultural—on the street level, our girls in the city kind of look out for each other, but you still see the Indigenous sex workers kind of in a little pack. Blocked together.

In a smaller city, there's support along the lines of, "You need clean rigs, girl?" "Do you need better, safer supply? I can help you with that." You see a lot of that—I don't want to say superficial fuckin' help, it's important help. If you know a safe supplier, that's amazing. If you know where I can get condoms at two in the morning, from a peer on this street, that's amazing, thanks for the help!

But that's surface help. It's not the help that so many, I was going to say Indigenous women but even non-Indigenous women, [need]: going that extra mile and looking at that emotional aspect. So many of our women suffer from extreme mental health issues, PTSD . . . how are these services looking at that?

We give free condoms, we give safer injection kits—yeah, we're doing a fucking amazing job, but how can we take that a step further to build these women up?

We're looking at the physical: we're giving you clean supplies, we're making sure you know where to go and get groceries, or detox.

But let's look at the whole of a person.

I think a lot of funders fund a project for a year: there's this grant money, and you can only go so far with grant money; you need to be able to prove the stats are there. People apply for these grants and money with good intentions, but they don't have the capacity to collect the data they need to continue or to prove that "there is a real need."

A lot of it is these former sex workers that start these little initiatives that—some amazingly turn into nonprofits!—but if you have a sex worker with minimal education who's a fierce advocate who applies for this money, she doesn't necessarily have the capacity or know-how to continue that once the money comes to an end.

Pick your battles. Where are you going to devote your energy? Is it to educating, and tearing down misconceptions? Focus where it matters. Too often we forget about why we wanted this grant money to begin with: it was for that woman, trying to find her voice and support. People get so caught up in all the functions and operations that we forget where our fire and passion comes from.

Right now, the work that I'm doing, my fire is burning bright. Because I'm in a space and organization that fosters that fire.

It's finding that, and when you find that passion, fuck it. You're needed. And when it's time to pass the torch, pass the fucking torch.

Different perspectives are needed, different worldviews are needed at that fucking planning table. Not just white sex workers. You're not the god of every sex worker on the fucking street. I've seen that so much. Yeah, you have a strong voice, people listen to you: you're fucking white.

They're gonna listen to you. But let's bring some Indigenous sex workers in here. Bring them to the table.

A lot of that, too, what I saw the barriers were—a lot of our girls were so fucking high, strung out—they wanted to speak and share but weren't in the space. That alone should tell you that her problems are far greater than those white sex workers at the table who can plan and look ahead, when survival for her is in this day. That meeting's on Friday? Fuck, that's three days from now, a lot can happen.

So then there's this idea that if she goes missing, or she gets murdered, "That's the choice she made." I was speaking at an awareness day for Missing and Murdered Indigenous Women, and there was a white male, and that was his view. I must have stood there for twenty minutes, trying to educate and get him to see from a different perspective: we don't choose this. We don't deserve what happens. And I had professors within proximity, who didn't say anything. I was so fucking mad. I was like, I needed your help.

But they taught me that you choose your battles. Where are you going to put your energy?

That's a hard-earned lesson: I had elders and teachers around me who found it amusing, because that was them too. You've got to pick your battles and channel where your energy is going to be best spent.

It's like those, you know, kids on those little leashes? It's like that. Their fiery little spirits, and I'm like, "Whoa, whoa, hold on. Come back, we're not going to run in the street. This is how we're going to go about it."

That's like with young activists. That was me, so many times, just ready to run.

I had my own healing journey: I ended up succumbing to alcohol, I lost my mother, I did a lot of trauma work, I did a lot of inner-child work. I got into this through counselors and going to women's sharing circles, AA, NA. It started out sharing. Women just started: "I really appreciate what you shared."

I started beading, doing craft work, and I would take it to Monday-night drum social, and then programs would ask, "Would you consider coming to teach a circle on how to bead?"

"Sure," and through that process, I'm talking to women—these are women who don't have their children—and I talk, and I share. "I remember when ..."

And they're like, "Are you fucking serious? You don't have custody of your kids? You struggle? I would never have guessed." It's being honest and learning to walk in your truth and being okay with your journey and all the lessons it has taught you.

That got me involved in peer support work. I started in the help-ing field as a peer support worker within the mental health world. As a peer support worker in street outreach, handing out supplies, because I had the lived experience. It wasn't so much my degree, it was that I had experience to be able to connect with the population. And that's why I think peer work is so fucking important.

But getting peers out there. Not just the white sex worker, not just the "proud to be a fucking sex worker" reclaiming her body. Let's get that one who doesn't like the tight-fitting clothes, who's out there and you don't know whether she's a boy or not, but she's out there and she's amazing at sucking dick. Let's get that one at the table. Let's get a diverse conversation happening.

That's how I started. It was just sharing my experience. I was at a MMIW [Missing and Murdered Indigenous Women] conference and talking about seeing an Indigenous sister get beaten and nobody helping. And then, people scoop you up. SWAN [Sex Workers and Allies Network] scooped me up. "You're a sex worker? We need an Indigenous person at our table."

It was really like that. And I don't think I'd call it out like that. People aren't even aware of when they're scooping up an Indian for that token representation, or they're in denial. Their intentions are good, they're trying to be as diverse as possible, but as the lone Indigenous person at a planning table where the mandate is already so clear—"This is what we are going to do for these sex workers, and we need you here"—you're walking into a box that's already built, and you have to be able to operate within that box.

It was hard in that sense.

If I had unlimited funding? I would create spaces. Spaces specific to Indigenous workers and excluding the white worker. We fight so hard to bring our Indigenous swers into the white sex work spaces and we fight so hard to help them feel comfortable in that space, because these are fucking sex workers. Fierce. "I'm a fucking whore and I'm fucking proud of it."

And I'm serious, fuck, if that's you, I'm right there with you. I don't give a fuck, I'll scream too. But! It's taken me many fucking years of trauma work and therapy to be in this space with you white sex workers. This Indigenous worker? She's not there. And supporting her to get to that Friday planning meeting in her own space where she has other sisters who are struggling the same way? Vital.

Indigenous sex work spaces.

Key, pivotal, at the top of that list.

I would then look at cultural helpers who are understanding of the struggles she's going through. Maybe it's an elder, their teachers, who has been down that path. And knows the girl's journey, is able to support her in that space. And just working on building them up, looking at them as a whole and working from an Indigenous worldview. Their self-esteem and self-worth is nowhere near where the non-Indigenous sex worker is at. I know that, I feel that.

It's not, "I need to buy for my kids": she doesn't have her fucking kids, they're wards of the Crown. She doesn't have a home.

There's a lot of barriers there. So creating a space specific for the Indigenous sex worker, which I have not seen yet. Is there one anywhere?

It's so much more complex. Look at how we serve mental health, how we serve the Indigenous person who has mental health issues: we're including a cultural component there; we're finally recognizing the importance of cultural competency, just within mental health. We're getting there.

Manon's Response

I agree that white sex worker activism spaces are extremely classist when it comes to the entry requirements of academic knowledge or scholastic experience. The smartest, best problem solvers are not necessarily the people this shit is the easiest for. It's probably the people who have had to come up with their own solutions to meet their needs. The fact that their priorities and methods are ignored time and again is infuriating.

Everyone at my club who was undocumented, for example, got fired when the manager found out I was involved in a union effort. One of the few Black dancers almost got fired as well. Those undocumented strippers were trading under the table with management for a safer place than the street to work. They didn't give a fuck about being an hourly-wage employee: how would they even be able to collect it, and what bank account would they put that check into? Because of their more vulnerable status in the club, they were also the ones who did extras more often, and usually for less money than what the white strippers would charge, which meant less of a tipout from them, because they made less. So there was an immediate "reason" for them to be fired.

I think many white pro-sex work activists in the US ignore the reality of Indigenous people, and often also undocumented sex workers, because it doesn't fit within the narrative of reclamation they have created. I really agree with Crystal's position that some of us just need to reclaim our sanity, dignity, or mental health. Not everyone needs to feel proud of doing or having done sex work; we need to feel proud of who we are.

I related a lot to Crystal's point about ancestral trauma in the blood as well, where you could grow up with two parents who are not abusive to you or themselves, have a place to live and go to school, food, clothes, and even go on family vacations, yet still *it's there*, passed down through stories and learned behaviors. Reflecting on my upbringing, I can see that it was an attempt to mimic a picture of stability that my parents never experienced. It was a barely-held-together image that shattered every time I tried to do the things my wealthy white peers did. In clawing my way toward a higher social class, eventually I was faced with a barrier too high to climb: fear of law and law enforcement, and poverty, and it effectively put me back in my place. So I was like, fuck it all, I will just do what I have learned is always a good idea: live in constant survival mode.

Another thing that resonated personally: as someone from a marginalized and specifically "undereducated" cultural group having insight into how white academics think about those "lower" than themselves, I have noticed that they so genuinely believe their own solutions to other people's problems, to the point that it can be almost impossible to give them a good argument for why they are wrong other than forcing them to either go live or closely witness the perspective of the people actually facing the problems that white academics are discussing. As a white-passing sex worker with some academic experience who is also from a marginalized cultural group, I have been invited into white academic sex work organizing spaces and have firsthand knowledge of how they already have what Crystal described as "a box already set up," and probably with instructions as well. My experience has often been that I am asked to participate ceremoniously as a token, used to further their goals exclusively, without even superficial interest in addressing the actual problems I was specifically there to help fix, oftentimes to the detriment of myself and those we were trying to help. I will mention this a third time on purpose: my one Black coworker almost got fired for visibly staying friends with me in the club after our manager found out I had been involved in some stripper union activities. All of the undocumented girls were fired immediately. If only he knew what those white stripper organizers had asked me to do for them *in the club*—we probably all would have been fired and replaced that night. That is why I agree with the need for exclusively Indigenous sex work and activist spaces, exclusively Black sex work and activist spaces, etc. Because while everyone absolutely needs to be at the white academic table, the white academic table also needs to just give their table and chairs to nonwhite, nonacademic organizers. Just trust the people who have lived the problem to be able to best solve the problem, and recognize that the only reason they haven't been able to execute their solutions is because there are no seats at the tables they need to be at in order to access the resources to do so.

Letter from a Social Worker

Aubrey

I had a visit with a foster teen today who's going to age out soon. She's had a hard time of it. As soon as she hit puberty, adult men discovered her and became the center of her universe. She wouldn't hear anything from workers about exploitation or abuse. She was mature, they loved her, and we were all just repressed and didn't understand. And, frankly, what could we offer her? Every adult in this kid's life, every single person who provided any kind of care for her, was drawing a paycheck off her and wouldn't be there without it. A pedophile would come pick her up, day or night, to tell her he loved her, but a social worker wouldn't answer her call after five p.m.

But she gets all the usual lines from workers and foster parents and therapists anyway–that she needs to have self-worth, that she isn't old or mature enough to understand, that she needs to think about her future, etc. And she refuses to hear any of it. Tell her she needs to develop job skills, or that the men who want to be with her are predators, and she would shut right down or start teenage-girl shrieking at us.

Her new line now is, "I don't care, it doesn't matter, I'm gonna run away and be a stripper." Anything I asked her about–school, friends, her future–she hit me with, "I don't care, it doesn't matter, I'm gonna run away and be a stripper."

Never work while you or the trick is high.

Always get the $$$ first. Put it away, but keep it close to you.

Use a condom for everything

even head.

Charge more.

Add-ons or changes cost extra. Get $ upfront.

Get someone to watch your back.

Make a plan.

DON'T BELIEVE THE HATE

We are mothers daughters sisters lovers workers wives & friends.

Hos R just as good as any body!

Tips and Tricks, by Leslie Bull

After hearing this a few times, I asked her, "What are you getting in math right now? Last I heard, it was a D."

"I don't care, it doesn't matter, I'm gonna—"

"Yeah, yeah, be a stripper. Well, unless you can get up to a C in math, you're gonna lose money hand over fist as a stripper."

We sat down and I pulled out a notebook and a pen and wrote down some numbers: stage fees, club fees, tipouts. Lap dances and percentages. I showed them all to her, then covered them up and asked her to add them up in her head. When she couldn't, I told her that meant the club owner was taking most of her money that night.

I took her shopping, and every time she put something in her basket, I asked, "Are you keeping track of how much everything costs?" She'd nod or shrug or tell me it was "probably fine" or make up a number that sounded close enough. I told her, "A stripper would know how much it all costs," and she finally, exasperatedly sat down and, with the help of the calculator on my phone, added it all up. Once she was done, I reminded her about tax, and with the loudest teenage groan, she started over.

After we'd gone through this routine a couple of times, she finally said, "It seems really unfair. Why do club owners get away with it?" And I introduced the word *whorephobia* to her, which I'm sure was fun for her foster mom when she got home. We got to talk about labor rights and what it means to be a contractor versus an employee.

Some of this was typical teenage stuff. She was trying to shock me, hoping to get the same pearl-clutching she'd reliably gotten from others. But I also think she was seriously mulling it over, and it gave me the rare opportunity to have a serious conversation with her.

When I told her that clients were constantly trying to scam strippers, she breezily told me, "I'm too smart to get scammed like that."

"Well," I reminded her, "apparently all it takes is an adult man on the Internet to say he loves you, and you'll head off to a hotel to show him your tits for free, like you did last month. So you're already getting scammed like that."

For the first time, for the first time, I heard it all click together in her mind as she said, "Oh, he was scamming me?"

I can't tell you how many times she'd been told that man had manipulated her, abused her, used her, that he didn't care if she was hurt, that he didn't care how she felt or if she was taken care of—and she would shut down cold to all of it. Because all those arguments were about her worth as a person, and that had no meaning to her yet. Why should it? If she had worth, why had all these horrible things happened to her? Why didn't anybody stick around to take care of her, unless they were being paid to do it?

But money made sense to her. It had meaning and relevance, was tangible and concrete and very present, because it was literally the only thing that ran her life. She generated paychecks for dozens of adults, paychecks that paid the rent of the placements she lived in. She was approaching eighteen and taking "life skills" classes about how she'd have to get a job to support herself soon. And she got to see all the things that kids who weren't in foster care got to have that she didn't, like vacations, or summer camp, or new clothes without being part of a church drive. Money mattered, and it mattered a lot more than her happiness or safety or worth. Finally, she could hear and understand me when I told her that adult men were trying to take something from her that mattered—and that she had every right to refuse to give it to them.

And stripping as a job made sense to her in a way other jobs didn't. Whenever adults talked to her about a future, a career, it was all abstract. But her sexuality wasn't abstract at all. It was here, right now, and valuable, right now. So talking to her about using her sexuality as an occupation, that it would require particular skills and come with particular hazards, was finally talking to her about something she could imagine and understand and make use of, not in a vague future, but today.

We also talked about how stripping can change your relationships. I told her I'd heard that stripping could make a person look at men differently, because so many of them, even ones who seemed nice, would try to mess with a stripper's boundaries or steal their time and money and services.

"Do strippers hate men?" she asked me.

"Not all of them," I said, "but I hear they're not as willing to put up with men. They see a lot more shitty ones, and they end up with higher standards."

"Then I won't strip. I don't want to hate men. Forget it," she said. But later, she brought it up again and said, "Stripping can be a lot of money, though, right?"

I told her, "Yeah, it could be. But only if you can learn to hustle men, which means you can't worry so much about what they think of you."

And she thought this over silently before saying, "Well ... maybe."

That "maybe" meant so much to me. It was the first time I'd ever heard her consider that something could matter more to her than finding a man who loved her. That something, anything, could replace the stranglehold men and their approval had on the center of her emotional life.

That conversation was hard to explain to coworkers and colleagues. They all thought I was coming at it from a harm reduction standpoint or using it as a "cool worker" technique. But I was legitimately hoping to help her weigh the pros and cons. Stripping seemed like a real option for her, one that might be helpful not just as a job, but as a way to rethink what mattered to her.

A big piece of my work is geared toward getting these kids reoriented to what a healthy, normal relationship is, letting them see that relationships don't have to be tenuous and manipulative and dangerous and transactional. And yeah, I want these kids to learn and seek and expect unconditional care and love. But in the meantime, because of the way they started, and because of the way predators can seek out and smell trauma and vulnerability, they're going to spend a much larger chunk of their life fending off people who want to exploit them.

I'd rather that girl learn to hustle better, learn to focus her hustle on her own long-term goals and achievements, than teach her that those skills are bad habits she needs to unlearn. They're bad habits in a good world, but she hasn't lived in that world yet. Yes, I want her to have an unconditionally loving relationship with a man (if that's what she wants), but I want her to be able to protect herself from men first. I want her to see her life, her needs, her skills and abilities and wants, as meaningful whether or not men approve. If she wants to be a stripper, that's not a peculiar and unfortunate deviation from a path toward developing and protecting her own worth; it's a straight shot toward it. Her body, her behaviors, her moods, her vulnerabilities and distress have been generating revenue for an entire government and nonprofit industry for her entire childhood. As an adult, why shouldn't she take that revenue back for herself? Why should she make less than we did off of her life? Why should we own it, and not her?

"Since painting my hottest art piece—a billboard calling out my violent rapist, the apathy of my club's managers, and LAPD's dismissal of the case—I feel launched into the movement. I have a talent for illustration, and it's my weapon in this fight."
Billboard by Monty Monster Slayer

Monty Monster Slayer

Do you remember the first time you learned that selling sex or performing sexy was a way to make money?

Knowing that sexy performances make money feels ingrained in our culture, because the "whore" is such a classic archetype in entertainment. My first time would definitely be performers in movies and TV; as a kid, it would be all animated babes such as Jessica Rabbit, Red Hot Riding Hood, and Holli Would. Then, as a preteen, through music that I felt reflected me, I idolized Dita Von Teese and Shakira's belly-dancing performances.

How did you find out, and what was your immediate reaction?

I absolutely loved them. They were so beautiful and so obviously powerful. I just wanted to be them.

Did you know it would be something that you would do for income at that point?

I didn't know that I would do it as income in the future. But I knew I'd make money drawing them! Being an artist was always my main goal.

When did you decide to trade sex/ualized services?

I tried dancing once in my hometown as soon as I could (eighteen), and I hated it because the patrons in my small town were broke as fuck. When I decided to move to LA and seriously pursue an art career, I knew I'd need more cash and started in Dallas to get there.

Did you first start working in a space or field where there were other sex workers around, or did you work in isolation? What was that like?
I started with stripping, so even though I was a square, artsy, small-town nerd, I could learn from all of the absolute stunners dancing in a hot club in the city.

Did you start out in a line of sex work you thought you would want to continue in, or were you treading water and learning with a plan to change it up? Club jumping counts here. Can you talk about why?
I really thought I could skirt the edges and just snatch up enough cash to continue pursuing my art goals. I've worked in Dallas, Vegas, and LA. I tried camming and sucked at it. I tried working in a dungeon and absolutely loved it. I wish I had just committed to it as my main career, because I ended up making just enough to float along and never unlocked my full earning potential for years.

What are some songs that were popular or that you loved when you first started doing sex work?
I started working in 2013, so Lana Del Rey was popular, and she had that sultry sugar-baby vibe that I was embracing, so my first song was "Off to the Races." Too bad Lana Del Rey turned out to be an asshole.

How has sex work—the way you do it, the way you think it's perceived and understood by outsiders, and the community of sex workers you know (if any)—changed since you started?
When I first started dancing, there was a big party vibe with the girls working, but I was really guarded and focused on my bag. When I returned to the club a few years later, the sex worker labor movement was so much louder, and there was a camaraderie among the dancers that I hadn't experienced before. Feminist language was adopted in the dressing room, and it felt like a sisterhood.

Do you feel like you're a part of a larger community of sex workers? In person or on the Internet?

I do feel like I'm part of a larger community of sex workers online, and most of my best friends in real life I've met in the club.

How do you see power dynamics play out in your community? What kind of workers are valued by other sex workers around you, and what kind of work is most valued?
There's some serious whorephobia, classism, and racism still rampant in our community; there's a group of sex workers who still believe that young, rich, white sugar babies are higher up in that hierarchy, but all the dope bitches know that veterans and woke babes taking money straight out of these old, rich white men's pockets and spending it better are the GOATs.

Do you feel involved in sex worker activism or organizing? Do you want to be?
Since painting my hottest art piece—a billboard calling out my violent rapist, the apathy of my club's managers, and LAPD's dismissal of the case—I feel launched into the movement. I have a talent for illustration, and it's my weapon in this fight.

What kind of organizing goals are prioritized by the sex workers around you?
I don't know of any organizers in real life, so I only really know of the loud ones online whose biggest concern is censorship on social media platforms.

Regardless of whether you're involved in activism or organizing, what do you see as important goals for us to work toward?
I think the most important goals are:
1. Sex work needs to be legalized. This work being seen as a criminal offense keeps workers who experience violence vulnerable. Lawmakers won't protect the victim when the law sees everyone involved as a criminal.
2. Getting the concept of "sex trafficking" and "sex work" confused isn't working out for us either. Sex work is work, and implementing laws like FOSTA/SESTA, EARN IT, and SISEA—whose intentions *state* that they're to remove online spaces that sex traffickers use to sell bodies—are just putting consensual

workers in danger, because workers use these spaces to find safe ways to make the money they need to survive.

What do you think are barriers to achieving those goals?
The biggest barriers that I can see are conservative lawmakers who don't consult the actual sex workers they're making laws about.

How are you coping with our current reality?
To deal with this reality, I'm using art to fight back in any way that I can: from making rude-ass illustrations telling my own story to having animations and movies in the works and making graphics for organizations that need to use imagery to grab their audience in five seconds or less.

What would you like to see from white sex workers moving forward? Individually and/or as a community and/or as organizers?
As a white-passing Latina and first-gen American, I can only offer advice to white sex workers that I need to keep in mind myself: Educate yourself on the white supremacy this country was founded on. Check the silent racism we were all raised in. You can't just claim that you're not racist, and appropriating BIPOC culture doesn't count as antiracist work. Read works by Black civil rights leaders, listen to the needs of BIPOC women, and pass the mic to BIPOC women.

Do you feel like having done sex work has given you certain skills that are useful in your day-to-day or non-swing life that others don't have? What are some of them? Are there disadvantages from sex work that also come up? If there are, will you elaborate on them?
I've learned some skills while dancing: I seem to keep topping sales in vanilla jobs! Huh, I wonder where I learned to finesse rich people? The disadvantage is that I have to really check that I'm not doing it in a way that's even remotely sexual. When I first got back into vanilla work, I thought that having my nipples show through my shirt wasn't a big deal. Oh, it's a big deal to squares. My current female boss actually called me out on bending over to wash my hands in the women's restroom because my ass was sticking out too much! I don't give these things a second thought, because I'm not consciously trying to be sexual (not to mention that I find literally nothing offensive with women's sex and sexuality, so it doesn't cross my mind as being intentionally rude); it's just how I

naturally move at this point. But the more I play by these conservatives' rules while keeping my mouthpiece in, the more money I rake in—to put into things that matter. Like a future in which women don't have to play small and conservative to make the money they need to survive.

Intimate Labor

Matilda Bickers

I have a hobby, a kind of maddening one. One of those things you do more to keep annoying yourself than because it's entertaining or refreshing.

I ask non-sex workers—particularly strip club customers, particularly female customers, particularly the ones who want to get onstage in a strip club and be the center of attention, the ones dancing in the aisle or claiming they could do anything better than us (when they can't take off their pants without falling over!)—whether they would ever give a lap dance, and when the answer is invariably "Oh no! I couldn't!" I offer increasing sums to see if they will change their minds. Like a six-year-old whose first tooth is loose, I can't stop nudging it, maybe pushing harder because of the twinge of pain.

When I started asking, I thought it was possible to get these people to conceive of sex work as work, as an act of physical labor that offers a better return on time and energy invested than an eight-hour workday, for example. I see these women fluffing their hair, trying to arch their backs and perform "sexy" to reclaim the attention of the men around them, and I wonder: *Why do it for free? Would you do it for money, what you give away so thoughtlessly?*

It started like on a slow Tuesday night, when there were nine customers and sixteen of us. The bulk of the customers were from a group of five, two men and three women, and one of the men had gotten snagged into VIP early on. The rest of us were desperately crowded around their table whenever we were offstage, hoping the remaining man would follow his friend's example. To be at the table, however, required engaging with his women friends.

Two of the more enterprising dancers had lured the women to the rack, where the women shrieked and required many motorboats in exchange for their meager dollars, then clambered onstage themselves to messily hop around with their pants around their knees and swing their heads, hair too short to whip. This seemed way too low an ROI to me, so I stuck with the guy, but the guy wasn't biting. He was enjoying the free attention and had zero intention of spending a dollar more than his alcohol cost.

My frustration mounted, watching these women take up so much space without offering compensation or even thought to whose space they were in, why we were there, and why they were there and why were they there? For the same reason men come, but rather than use our attention to make themselves feel good, they play-performed aspects of *our lives* to get attention to make themselves feel good. In the process, they redirected what little attention there was in the club to themselves, rather than to the people whose existence and presence made this space a possibility.

Nine dollars and five stage sets later, the women returned, breathless and pleased with themselves. I didn't have any other prospects of making money, so I threw caution to the wind.

"What would it take to get you onstage for real? Or into the lap dance room?"

Clearly, they were coveting every bit of attention and begrudging every dollar spent, even when it wasn't theirs. Why not put it out into the open? You desperately want something we have, but do you even know what that is? Do you think about *why* it is?

The answer was a horrified, shrieking laugh from each.

"No!"

"No, never!"

And finally, "Twenty *thousand* dollars. That's what I would give a lap dance for!"

"Seriously?" I stared at her blankly. Twenty thousand dollars is not actually engaging with the reality of *work* at all. "I make my electric bill in three minutes. My phone bill in nine. How long do you work to cover your bills? You would never?"

Inspired by this idiocy, the other two set astronomical values on the sight of their bare breasts, their asses grinding against denim—values they clearly didn't actually assign to themselves, as they'd *just* been flashing the club for free.

I was hooked now, fascinated by the cognitive dissonance, so I kept asking, "How much money would it take to get you in VIP? Would you do a lap dance for your electric bill? What if you made in three hours what it takes you two weeks to make at your actual job?" Unspoken: *Are you able to engage with the reality that this—for you a leisure spot, a place to relax—is actually a workplace and that your rest is created by our work? Can you imagine yourself in our position?*

I've asked this of many people now, and there is *rarely* an acceptance of these terms. Even women who were just getting fingerbanged by a stranger onstage for free—my club encouraged us to involve female customers in our shows—would declare themselves too good to grind on a dick through denim for any amount of money, though some claimed that they would become strippers and make ten thousand dollars a night just onstage. But lap dances? Grinding on a stranger's dick? The inclusion of payment in the equation moved that public nudity and sex from hilarious, edgy recreation to . . . something they could not even contemplate. Sex *work!* An unimaginable destination one can never return from.

I retired from dancing (into whoring, which is in some ways very much like retirement and in some ways even more exhausting), but my curiosity stayed sharp. I began asking my non-sex-working friends. Perhaps actually knowing a sex worker on a personal level—knowing the freedom I have to move slowly and spend time doing things that matter to me but pay nothing—would make a difference to their ability to imagine this other possibility.

I repeated the initial explanations I'd offered to the drunkles. "Think about your bills and having your phone bill in three minutes. Think about having your electric bill paid three minutes after that. Think about being able to make your rent in hours instead of weeks. Would you do it?"

It didn't work very well. I put the question in those terms to try and make it less abstract to my circle of acquaintances, but the very concept of performing a sexual service for money was too fantastical: the apparent absurdity of my request outweighed the sheer relief and security offered by making in minutes or hours or days what it would otherwise take weeks and months to accrue. The responses of those first three girls at the club were repeated ad nauseum.

Some hooker friends of mine were similarly fascinated, and the question spread, but the responses stayed the same insulting and hilarious "A *hundred thousand dollars*, and he has to be hot!" or "I'm not grinding on some nasty old man." We all had at least one friend say she was going to make a Seeking Arrangement profile but she only wanted a sugar daddy who would give her eight thousand dollars a month and not want sex–or that she didn't even *need* to make a Seeking Arrangement profile because that's simply the kind of man she attracts.

Even people I expected better from would settle on some absurdly high number that negates the point of the question, valuing some ephemeral or imaginary virtue or integrity above paid bills and security.

I get it. Many people are in a financial position that makes the idea of trading a sexual or sexualized service (like a lap dance) for money a hilarious fantasy. The concrete reality of cash, with all its possibilities, has been so separated from their day-to-day lives that it's more imaginary than anything, a series of virtual transactions that bear only a passing connection to their own actions and options.

I think this may be the inverse of the delusion clients cling to so fondly: that we do this because we love sex, and not because we need money. *Because* non-sex working women set such an absurdly high premium on sex for sale, clients are able to tell themselves that we do it because we love it. Even in situations where it should be obvious that it's all about the Benjamins, baby.

We sit on the edge of the bed, and I watch him get dressed. He's wearing ratty, yellow-stained Y-fronts that sag in back. The bulk of his belly, all hard fat that doesn't hide the hernia that pops out when he strains–which he does a lot during sex–leaves little to be seen of his thighs. Just enough room for his hands to rest.

"So why do you do this?" he asks, stretching to pull socks up his scrawny legs.

I'm having an off day, something that happens more when I'm stressed about money and tired. My curse as a sex worker, service industry worker, and functional human being has always been an inability to monitor and control my emotions and thus my mouth.

"Money!" I respond brightly.

"Not sex?"

I look at him blankly.

"A lot of these girls, they love sex. They just love sex so much. They do it for the sex, because it feels so good."

My foul mood doesn't lift, exactly, but the fantasticalness of this eighty-year-old—swollen stomach, popping intestinal hernia, black gums, a black, furred tongue (both of which he insisted on inflicting on me through forty-five minutes of cunnilingus, during which I imagined my vagina turtling into my body, pulling desperately away from the bacterial vaginosis his tongue was inevitably spreading, as no one with a tongue that color should be touching it to other people!)—this eighty-year-old man talking earnestly about the pleasures of sex with him as a reason for having sex with him, it makes my chest light. I struggle to hold back a hysterical giggle.

"That too," I agree. "I love sex. It's so wonderful. It's so"—I can't stop myself—"sexual."

He nods like this is deep wisdom and not an inane platitude to appease a paying customer, and I'm not surprised, because when he asked me how many orgasms I had and I said, "Oh, at least eight," he smiled and said, "Good," with no sense of irony. Clients like him are difficult only because of the repulsive physical condition of their bodies: the performance aspect of my job is already halfway done for me by their own determined ability to see only what pleases them.

I started thinking about this again because someone I am friendly with wanted to get into fetish work. She asked for support and advice. I suggested a very kind, laid-back client of mine, an ideal, gentle, and low-stakes introduction into something as intimidating as sex work. She accepted but, I guess, had imagined that fetish work didn't actually involve sexual/ized contact. When I got back to her with his interest and details on what our sessions were like, she said she wasn't up for that: too extreme.

Despite more than half-expecting this after years of people flinching from the very idea, I was still surprised and irritated: *You approach me about something I do, to ask me to help you do it, but when it comes down to it, you somehow fancy yourself above it? Your precious, unemployed feet are too good to be jacked off to? You need money, and you approached me for help doing what I do: what did you expect?*

Well, not having to touch a penis, clearly. Something more along the lines of modeling, with zero interaction. Just being observed? Maybe no ejaculate involved?

Obviously, not everyone wants to or can do sex work, in the same way that not everyone can be a professional ball player or an opera singer or an astronaut. I'm grateful for this! The market is glutted as it is; adding more workers into the mix when there is a fairly finite pool of clients is stressful.

At the same time, I can't help but see this as just another facet of the idea that "Sex is too important for women to ever have it for money." *For free*, certainly. For free, with a stranger you met at a bar while drunk? Sure. For free, with the man who fully supports you and your kids? Of course. (But *is* that free?) All kinds of free sex are legal and, depending on the part of the world you're in, fairly acceptable.

Add money, however, and the very people flashing their tits and picking up OkCupid dates are suddenly put off by the idea of being intimate with a stranger. "I would do it for fifty thousand dollars, and he has to be hot," one woman told me, as if the boyfriend next to her was some teen idol. The sheer number of women who will only have sex with paragons of beauty for piles of money—while caressing the shoulders of very unfortunate-looking men they have only just met—would be astounding if it weren't so predictable. The same politicians who maintain a woman's right to choose what to do with her body will absolutely balk when it comes to choosing to make money with her body through sex. Sex is intimate! Sex is meaningful! Sex with people for money will degrade your inherent worth and render you worthless.

"Worthless" may sound like a rhetorical flourish, but the sheer number of murdered sex workers, tallied up at the end of every year for December 17 and inevitably lengthened by another two or ten bodies before December 31, covers pages. Last December 17, it was seven pages of names, and those are only the dead whose bodies have been found. Sex workers and civilians alike know what a whore is worth: not even worth stopping serial killers over.

After I quit dancing, I had a job with the government, briefly. I was hired to operate a hotline for sex workers, to answer questions about sex worker rights. I believed in that job and that goal more than I'd believed in any job before, but I learned fast that no one had any intention of letting me do it. I was a receptionist: I answered phones and mailed out complaints and delivered mail. Any attempt at doing anything else–for example, my job description–got me a slapdown from my boss. Even being a minute late stepping off the elevator to the tenth floor after lunch earned me scathing emails and lectures. I couldn't get up to stretch between hours sitting at a computer. My union steward told me frankly that he couldn't stop looking at my chest, and who do you complain about your union steward to? HR stared at me blankly and said nothing could be done. To go from the exploitative autonomy of the club to this job where the pay was so pitiful I couldn't even stop whoring and then not be allowed to do the only thing I wanted to do, the only reason I was even *there*, was heartbreaking. My former belief humiliated me. Clients have hurt me and customers have thrown pints of beer at me (okay, *one* pint) while I was onstage, but none of those things were as painful–in the moment or in memory–as my three months failing to run a hotline.

I whore but I have an on-the-books job now. I spend shifts lifting two-hundred-pound men in and out of wheelchairs, because the facility doesn't want us to waste the time it takes to use the lifts. My women coworkers make less than the men, and on top of that we're harassed and belittled: even my favorite resident calls us "cows" when he's sulky. Last night I was elbow-deep in a giant pile of shit that the person with the poop fetish deliberately smeared all over his wheelchair and clothing and bed, the person the male staff refuse to interact with *because they can*. Not only am I sexually harassed, I have to wash and fold the clothes of the people who harass me. My job is to take care of them, and my job has no interest in taking care of me in return. They cut our benefits and remind us to do self-care.

Both of my jobs deal heavily with genitals and body functions few people are comfortable discussing openly in public, and consequently both of my jobs earn low respect from the general public and often our own clientele. (Inextricable from both is the fact that both jobs are historically considered to be in the "feminine" realm of care work.) But the pay differential is huge and bizarre, a symptom of late-stage capital-ism: when I do work that keeps people physically healthy, I make nothing. Were it not for whoring, I would be impoverished, unable to afford to live within thirty miles of my job, unable to take care of my dogs or myself, unable even to afford food or car insurance.

I love orgasms as much as anyone, but providing them *should not* pay so exponentially more than keeping people's bodies healthy. I'm not saying that sex workers should be paid less: I think what I charge for the service of making you feel cherished and adored for an hour is not a penny less than I've earned. But caregiving–feeding people, cleaning people, keeping their skin from breakdown, and giving them medications and monitoring their health–should weigh higher than giving orgasms. It should weigh higher than banking. It's one of those jobs like "janitor" and "garbage collector" that keeps everything going without any acknowledgment.

And no, neither is low skill. Neither whoring nor caregiving can be done well by just anyone at all: while indoor whoring requires a specific level of pleasure performance, wiping asses and moving people and brushing their teeth and keeping them alive day to day (*and* appearing happy enough while you do it that your client doesn't feel frightened or uncomfortable) is a tiring emotional and physical performance. You have to be gentle with the bodies of ill and dying people, and if you're any kind of ethical, you have to treat them with dignity. Brushing someone else's teeth is a whole other level of weirdly intimate, on par with–but not as unpleasant as!–the dreaded Deep French Kiss. And you don't want to make it like a DFK for them: some foreign object shoved in their mouth and poked around.

As I stood in the laundry room one night, resting my aching back against one of the warm, vibrating dryers and folding the underwear of the resident who constantly corners me and hits on me, I thought about this construct that trading sex or sexualized services is degrading. I thought, "I'd rather be face-deep in the long and unkempt pubes of one of my more grotesque regulars, with the knowledge that I'll be free of him in an hour, with a quarter of my rent in hand, than stand here folding the underwear of a man who is very clear that he fantasizes about me being face-deep in *his* pubes as I cringe out of his reach for eight to twelve hours straight, all for minimum wage." Not only is it emotionally and mentally exhausting, it's also physically damaging. In terms of long-term harm, care work is far worse than six hours in stripper heels.

This is something that I think only other working-class people or sex workers or working-class sex workers can possibly get: sex with straight cis men is often work, and being sexy is usually a performance, whether or not either are done for money.

Maybe we're less wedded to this metaphysical concept of sex-as-meaningful because working-class women, women of color, trans women, and sex workers—all of us *already* don't meet the Western standard for chastity and womanhood. We fall short: our work historically enabled the leisure and chastity of middle- and upper-class women, while our existence allows them to construct their understanding of proper womanhood in opposition to us. We're already treated as sexual commodities for men, and because we fall short of proper womanhood, the move to sex as labor is perhaps less unimaginable, less of a stretch. In many ways, it's already been forced on us. Having to perform attractive pleasure for someone we can't stand, or simply having to live through someone else's pleasure—it does make getting something back from the constant demands of heterosexual white supremacy appealing.

If you're from a middle-class background, if you've only ever worked in a nine-to-five, making a salary that comes in and out of your life through a series of virtual transactions, if you've never had to stand for hours on your feet, breaking your back for minimum wage or suffering through the pawing of some creep to keep your job, then, yeah, I can see how the physical-labor side of sex would remain invisible. Sex is packaged to women along with *Romance!* as our raison d'être: we are *supposed* to see sex as inherently magic and meaningful, the ultimate intimacy. Even if you're not from a Christian-patriarchy family, we all know people like Jane Villaneuva's *abuela*, telling us virginity (a social construct to begin with) is precious and unless we save it for the right man and moment, we're trash. We're taught to find pleasure in being desired but not taught about desiring. All of this presented as natural.

All of that makes sense, yet I'm still a little bewildered by the insistence on commodified sexual intimacy as uniquely intimate and undesirable. I cleaned up after the poop fetishist at my respectable job for eight hours. At one point, my face was two feet away from his bare ass as he shit himself. I know he wants to get a reaction; he once put a butt plug in before he pooped and laughed. Not only is this *not* something I would do for any of my sex work clients, but if I *were* to work with scat fetishists, I would be in a cleaner space with more control and my clients would not deliberately create a mess for me. My inability to control the situation or react without reprisal makes it worse; my superiors have decided to let him get away with this harassment, and we have to take it or look for other jobs. *That's* degrading. I don't believe in

using "degraded" for people, but working with this person is the closest
I have come.

When my civilian respondents shriek out astronomical fantasy sums
as their price for a sexual service, they are reminding me that they have
more worth than I do, both financially, with jobs that cocoon them from
the reality that there are shittier jobs than sex (literally!), and socially,
having not damaged their integrity with anything as base as sex for pay;
by refusing to honestly engage with my question or simply saying they
can't imagine it, they're reinforcing that power differential.

This is not to say that sex work is not sometimes awful or humiliating or painful: it is. However, it's very far from the only job that can be
those things, and it most certainly offers the best pay potential. I'm not
offering some long-winded defense of it (Defend sex workers and our
rights? Yes. The industry? Never), but I am demanding that we reassess
what qualifies as intimate, what qualifies as intimacy, what qualifies as
degrading, and, most of all, what qualifies as *work*.

Janis Luna

Do you remember the first time you learned that selling sex or performing sexy was a way to make money?
I'm pretty sure the first time I learned about selling and performing sex was via watching *Jesus Christ Superstar*, which was one of my very favorite movies growing up. I was absolutely captivated by Mary Magdalene, and remain so, and I was equally captivated by the relationship between Mary and Jesus. I was raised pretty strictly Catholic (baptized, CCD, communion, confirmation, the whole thing) and am Latine on one side of my family and pretty traditionally New York Italian on the other, so I'm kind of amazed that *Jesus Christ Superstar* was part of my cultural lexicon at all. (I guess my dad, who loves musicals, was more of a theater buff than a scripture buff, for which I am eternally grateful.) Anyway, Mary really stuck with me, even though apparently scholarly articles claim that Mary the prostitute is a fictionalized amalgamation. I refuse to believe it, and I'm happy sticking with my head canon: Mary was a sex worker and his most trusted disciple, and Jesus was a queer brown anticapitalist abolitionist who loved, respected, and revered whores.

When did you decide to trade sex/ualized services?
I came to stripping late, at about twenty-six or twenty-seven, and have

dabbled in a very small handful of dates outside the club with trusted coworkers of mine. (My experience in this area is so limited that I try to be as careful as possible with regard to not overstating it or appropriating folks who have more long-standing full-service experience than I do.) I started because I'd started working at sixteen, first in my local grocery store and then, for a very long stint, in various hospital administrative jobs, which were basically giving me mental health problems, a drinking problem, and sucked all the time and energy out of my day. Stripping was really scary and anxiety inducing at first: I'm stiff onstage and not a great improvisor, so it was a steep learning curve. After my first three months, I got another hospital job. Then I decided to go back to grad school to become a therapist, and out of necessity I went back to the club, because as a social work grad student I had to work three full days a week as an unpaid intern and had no other way of making money. I started working at a different club (both divier and also more racially, ethnically, and body-shape diverse), stuck it out, made some wonderful friends, and would still be dancing today if it hadn't been for COVID. I did a strip tease to "Big Spender" in high school during an extremely undersupervised "Night of Scenes," though, so when my friends found out I had started stripping, none of them were surprised.

How has sex work—the way you do it, the way you think it's perceived and understood by outsiders, and the community of sex workers you know (if any)—changed since you started?

People are talking about sex work a lot more since I started, especially since COVID hit. There are more people talking about, and probably running, OnlyFans accounts; simultaneously, there are also more people using OnlyFans as a punch line or the butt of boring, unoriginal jokes. There are more sex workers struggling—which in NYC is alarming, because the club scene, in my experience and in the words of my coworkers, had already been deteriorating in this city over the course of my time dancing: there were simultaneously *more* people coming to the club and *less* money being spent. Yet at the same time, because sex work is so ubiquitous in terms of media representation (for better or, usually, for worse), the myths of it being easy money just seem to be perpetuated.

Do you feel like having done sex work has given you certain skills that are useful in your day-to-day or non-swing life that others don't have?

What are some of them? Are there disadvantages from sex work that also come up? If there are, will you elaborate on them?

Being a sex worker has absolutely made me a better therapist and comrade when it comes to mutual aid work and organizing. Sex work has given me insight into so much about human nature. It has helped me understand, in an extremely embodied and experiential way, power dynamics, privilege, and oppression—both as it plays out in the club with clients and with other sex workers along the intersections of our identities. It has helped me sit with others in a calm, warm, and nonjudgmental way. It has taught me grit, determination, and self-respect, not only via my own personal experiences, but in witnessing how the women and nonbinary people I've danced with keep showing up, at the club and for each other, night after night, no matter what our piece-of-shit, exploitative managers or completely out-of-line clients try to throw at us.

Where do you hope to be in five years? Don't let the current state of reality hold you back: what's your ideal world that you want to be living in in five years?

In five years, I'll be running my own private sex-worker-affirming therapy practice and supervising other sex workers turned therapists. I want to create a working environment where current and former sex worker therapists and educators can start their own practices in a way that protects them from the economically exploitative conditions that most newbie social workers and clinicians emerge into: fee-for-service jobs that pay less than minimum wage despite us already having two years of unpaid work under our belts and astronomical student-loan debt breathing down our necks. It is my intention to create a nonhierarchical practice that is self-sustaining, one that not only allows us to offer services that are accessible to people regardless of income or insurance status, but that also allows our therapists to make a livable wage that is not only sustainable for them but allows them to thrive in this work. And I want the model of this practice to extend nationwide.

1099 Problems

Susan Elizabeth Shepard

The worst thing to ever happen for stripper labor rights was for worker misclassification to somehow take center stage. The massive misdirection that has resulted from dancers simply trying to use one of the only tools available to them—lawsuits alleging they've been wrongfully classified as independent contractors—has resulted in a deep divide among strippers about what's better: to be an employee or to be an independent contractor. The fight over worker status, where the self-determination of an independent contractor is pitted against the labor protections of an employee, has obscured what Americans have started to realize about health care: rights aren't any kind of rights at all when they are tied to employment.

Every shitty thing that happens to dancers classified as independent contractors (not having the right to sue for discrimination or harassment, leaving the club having paid more to work than they earned, having a DJ expect 10 percent) or employees (extensive, sometimes racist dress codes, strict schedules, clubs keeping a large percentage of private dance sales) is also being done to dancers under the opposite classification.

These club policies have not been changed by three decades of nearly uniformly successful lawsuits resulting in judgments and settlements against clubs. These lawsuits have been lucrative for employment lawyers, and certainly some of those lawyers have truly believed this was a way

After Work, by Cecilia Bahls

to advance the cause of stripper labor rights. But still, the result is that while club policies stay the same, you've now got firms using personal injury techniques to get dancer plaintiffs.

Now, these lawsuits wouldn't have been so successful if the clubs weren't so clearly in violation of labor law, which is why it's so frustrating to see dancers accept a club's explanation that rising house fees are "because of lawsuits." Clubs have a lot invested in getting dancers to believe that IC status is to their benefit, and they seem to be bent on proving the point by making employee status especially bad by imposing astronomical increases in house cuts, limiting schedules, and lengthening the rule sheet. But what helps them more than anything is how much being totally, legally, properly classified as an employee can suck—and how bosses can mistreat workers in exactly the same ways whether they're getting 1099s or W-2s.

In either case, good fucking luck improving working conditions with a complaint to a state or federal agency.

If one was operating from a belief that labor laws in this country would be enforced, there would be reason to believe that employee status was worth pursuing, since everything from the right to organize to the right to sue for discrimination is tied to it. Back when Lily Burana and her coworkers sued the Mitchell Brothers Theater, they saw it as a blow against the then-new practice of charging dancers to work, and in the present day, activist dancers who file multiple misclassification claims against clubs claim it's a necessary step in improving working conditions.

The dancers who would prefer independent contractor status because they want a minimal paper trail and maximum freedoms are not persuaded. It's not just astroturfing by club owners that makes dancers leery of W-2 status. For some of them, something as routine as using a 1099 for credit card tips is to risk too much evidence of having ever worked in a strip club, so they simply don't work in the clubs where credit card payouts are issued with a record. Dancers who don't have documentation or authorization to work in the US also have excellent reason to avoid clubs that do things by or on the books. It's the same kind of tradeoff that workers on the margins have always made in choosing society, the law, or the boss: stigma, criminalization, or exploitation.

Back when this category of worker was invented at the time of the New Deal (by direct-sales companies like Avon's predecessor and the

Fuller Brush Company), the basics of the law were that in exchange for paying their own payroll taxes, workers got to set their own schedule and wouldn't be told how to work or how much to charge. Long before ride-share companies followed suit and started spending millions to run roughshod over state and local regulations in order to put taxi companies out of business with a workforce they did not pay, strip clubs figured out they no longer needed to have dancers on the payroll or be on the hook for the associated taxes and workers' comp insurance.

In the late 1980s, San Francisco clubs stopped paying dancers and started charging them a fee to work, in the model of other independent contractor jobs like hairdressers in salons. This could have been simple: Want to tell workers when to be there and how to work? They're on payroll. Willing to let them work when and how they want? They're contractors. Some clubs managed to do the latter.

But most clubs simply could not stop telling the dancers what to do! Almost immediately after clubs stopped paying dancers, the first misclassification lawsuits were filed by dancers who knew it wasn't legal for clubs to take a part of their tips (and the ways clubs do this range from the minimally painful five-dollar flat house fee to taking upwards of 50 percent of private dance sales to actually making dancers turn over their stage tips to be counted), not pay them, but still tell them how, when, and where to work. Misclassification class actions in federal courts have resulted in multimillion-dollar settlements: $13 million from the Spearmint Rhino, $6 million from Scarlett's, $4 million from Flashdancers. The current record is $15 million from Rick's in New York, and in an order on that case, the judge noted that at that time, only two federal rulings had ever not found that an employment relationship existed.

All of these lawsuits never resulted in clubs either converting dancers to employees en masse or substantially changing their business practices. Then, in 2018, the California Supreme Court found in *Dynamex v. Superior Court* that a delivery company had misclassified its drivers. The *Dynamex* opinion established a drastically stricter standard for worker classification, and all of a sudden, a misclassification lawsuit had the potential for real consequences. The subsequent legislation and ballot initiatives are changing so rapidly that any summary here would be guaranteed to be outdated in three months. The biggest and latest development was the passage of Prop 22 in November 2020, a ballot initiative that specifically carved out an exception for ride-share drivers from employee status—and that was ruled unconstitutional by a state judge in August 2021. It has remained in effect as it moves through appeals.

Dynamex coincided with the biggest, most frequently sued strip club chain in the state, Déjà Vu, putting dancers on payroll, a move the chain made in settling a lawsuit. In October of 2018, signs went up in dressing rooms saying that all clubs in California were about to convert dancers to employees because "entertainer attorneys and the State of California are suing nearly ALL other California adult clubs as well."[1] "Entertainer attorneys" had been suing Déjà Vu since at least 1994, but it wasn't until *Dynamex* that Déjà Vu (and another California chain, Spearmint Rhino) agreed to reclassify dancers as part of a settlement.

Because Déjà Vu owns clubs to the point of having a near-monopoly in San Francisco and has multiple clubs in other cities in California, dancers can be forgiven for believing this was true. It wasn't; there were and are independent clubs in California still classifying dancers as contractors, including Star Garden, where strippers went on strike and filed for a union election in 2022. But the strippers took to social media to show similar signs from Sacramento to San Diego saying the same kinds of things: they were going on payroll, and, by the way, they'd be keeping a lot less of their tips, getting fewer hours, and being issued uniforms. (The fact that these signs basically said these punitive changes were the result of lawsuits is at the center of another class action alleging that the changes were retaliatory.) Déjà Vu framed these as inevitable consequences of employee status, but they weren't; they were the choices that Déjà Vu made about how to implement employee status. The company engaged the services of Stormy Daniels as a spokesperson, and the *Los Angeles Times* published an op-ed Daniels wrote about how bad employee status was for dancers.

Dancers rightfully freaked out about the change. Without diminishing the hit to their income, though, here's the thing: cutting into dancers' sales, messing with their hours, imposing new and ridiculous rules? From my perspective as someone who worked at a Vu club once and walked out of another in disbelief when the manager told me they kept seven dollars from every twenty-dollar table dance, they already did a lot of this when the dancers were contractors. Déjà Vu chooses to run its business that way because taking a big cut from strippers' sales is part of its business model. The worker classification of the strippers is incidental. Workers are treated badly because, fundamentally, in this system, work is bad!

What of the independent clubs? A lot of them really wouldn't be able to stay in business if they had to start paying everyone. But that doesn't make them unique as businesses. At least the strip clubs turn a profit the way they do it now. Uber sure as hell can't say that! Its business model absolutely relies on not paying the people who work through its app, and it has yet to become profitable, losing $8.5 billion in 2019 because of its subsidies to drivers as it undercuts cab companies.

The problem for dancers and most other service industry independent contractors is that getting employee status rarely helps them—and can hurt them. Employee status grants protections in theory like the benefits of a minimum wage paycheck, workers' comp, and discrimination protections, but it isn't a magical hedge against being treated illegally nor against having a business take part of a worker's tips. There's barely enforcement for the employee protections that exist, anyway. Waged workers risk their jobs when they try to report harassment or wage and hour violations, and it's very hard to prove retaliation from an employer. If you're still going to have to file a complaint to access your rights, they don't really feel like rights, just privileges that people who can pay lawyers and are willing to set a small part of their lives on fire can have.

Employee status also doesn't do the one thing most dancers would want: stop clubs from taking their money. At clubs where dancers are on payroll, they may have to make a sales quota, adhere to a set schedule or be fined for missing a shift, or pay out half or more of their earnings to the club. Of course, dancers called independent contractors may have to do all of these as well. Many dancers wish clubs would truly just treat them as independent contractors and quit telling them when and how to work. But there's no enforcement mechanism in place for that. You literally can't go to court to make an employer stop charging you a house fee or stop putting you on a schedule—you can just go to court to say they owe you back wages because they were treating you like an employee.

How well a dancer is treated isn't a consequence of worker status. It's a consequence of who owns the club.

This means that across clubs there's a vast difference in the way dancers experience being contractors or employees. Working conditions can be as different across clubs as working at a Chipotle can be from hostessing at a Morton's, and that, combined with the mobility and transience of dancers, is a big obstacle to building solidarity among them. There's a reason that, twenty-four years after the dancers at San

Francisco's Lusty Lady peepshow organized, it's still the only example anyone can think of when they suggest dancers "get a union." It's the only time it's happened! It had a setup so unique as to be unreplicated anywhere else so far: as workers in a peepshow, the dancers interacted with each other closely and frequently in a common performance area (rather than being dispersed out on the club floor, mingling with customers), the number of performers working was relatively small, and they were already employees receiving a paycheck.

When will a club unionize again? Seizing on the upshot of employee status, in California a group called Soldiers of Pole quickly informed dancers that they may have lost half their money, but they'd just gained the right to form a union. Contractors can't technically do so, nor can they collectively bargain in the traditional sense (although wildcat strikes and direct pickets are options for everyone!). Soldiers of Pole—which changed its name to Strippers United—helped organize the Star Garden dancers in 2022, leading to a blitz of media coverage and, as of September 2022, a pending union election as dancers head for a sixth month on the picket line.

As someone who unionized a small newspaper along with my coworkers only to have it shut down by its corporate owners, my pessimistic view is that the only way to organize is to get each club to organize—but more than one will have to do it at the same time to avoid simply being shut down to squash organizing. Remember, the reason the Lusty Lady closed wasn't because of fat union contracts. It was because Déjà Vu cofounder Roger Forbes bought the building America's only union strip club was in and jacked up their rent!

Conventional organizing assumes secrecy at the outset, where workers start out by talking with each other quietly and try to keep that *a big secret* from the bosses. Once you've got enough people on board to either ask for recognition or an election, you can finally go public. I'd like to think this could happen at a club. What we've seen instead have been social-media-based efforts that reach a large but diffuse audience—you might get a hundred dancers interested in organizing, but they're spread out over twenty clubs.

That's been an issue for the dancers taking part in the New York City stripper strike and Portland stripper strike (now the Haymarket Pole Collective); as soon as clubs see what they're up to, they're subject to no longer having their names put on the schedule. Both of these actions had the goal of getting clubs to stop their well-known racist hiring and scheduling practices and were born on social media—strippers are very, very good at Instagram. It's a fast and effective way to get word out to other dancers, and it managed to really move forward the ways strippers engage with sex work activism.

It also flattens nuance and is a terrible place to explain the complexities of labor law as it is applied to strippers, and a lot of confusion has ensued from the use of the word *strike* to describe something that has not ever been an actual organized work stoppage. While solid branding, when dancers hear about a strike, they think: Work stoppage. No money. Picket lines. It can be scary! And if the first they hear of it is on social media, with no context, it can splinter rather than unify dancers.

To really get workers on the same page, you need circumstances like those at the Lusty Lady—a regular group that spends a lot of time together and that isn't too large and isn't itinerant. At clubs with fifty-plus dancers, where new ones start and quit every week, it's much more difficult to develop those personal relationships that successful organizing drives are built on.

That isn't to say it's impossible. A few years ago, the idea that small newspapers in Wyoming and southwest Washington state would form unions would have seemed improbable, let alone a union for Burgerville workers. The resurgence of labor actions is real. At some point, dancers at a club, regardless of how they're classified, will use direct collective actions to force owners to give them concrete things like equitable scheduling, no fines, and the ability to set their own prices. This appears to be what happened at Star Garden—it's a small, tight crew of dancers who made their move when many of them were outraged by specific management actions that threatened their safety.

That is how they could improve working conditions, and it's only acquired by collective action, regardless of worker classification. Having that actual bargaining power and a seat at the table is far more consequential than having the right to file paperwork with the EEOC. If there's one thing that strippers do understand, it's that you don't get what you don't ask for.

Note

1   The sign can be viewed at https://drive.google.com/ file/d/13_DQQgutSE2z3V1UmHJaCN8gJypDpJaS/view.

Metatopia: Imagination beyond Dystopia

Dee Lucas

This being among the last moments of the year two thousand and nineteen, there is plenty to say—plenty we've all said and all heard—about
how the world of today is *nothing* like what we were made to expect as
children ... and yet, it is precisely that.

There is plenty to say about coming of age in a society buckling
under endless terror, gun violence, and financial destabilization. I
remember what class I was in during 9/11, yes. My schools experienced
active shooters and possible bombers before it was common enough
that the whole world considered it a crisis. I heard the discussions about
the government and the economy as I washed dishes at night, and not
long after, I found myself an eighteen-year-old runaway from a home
where the narratives of patriarchy, racism, and capitalism played out as
"family drama." And not long after that, I was a tryhard twenty-year-old
who, with no family support, was throwing themselves into the fray
with a do-or-die willingness to succeed. "Success" at that time meant
consistently avoiding poverty, and so years later when—at the end of,
what, two? three? recessions—debt came knocking at my door, I, like so
many others, turned to sex work.

I also grew up before the Internet was a permanent fixture, before
companies could know about you what they know now, all the better

In the Future, by Rambling Hooker

to target you with bespoke exploitation. I grew up under adults entirely hypnotized by the plastic promises of the American Dream, knowing already that they as adults had lost sight of something I knew as a child. That life was full of magic. That the Earth could speak. That without love, spirit, and imagination, the world became dark and poisonous.

I did not know, at the time, that I was growing up into a world that people would call a "dystopia" without a hint of irony.

I did not know as a child that the lines between make-believe and reality did not quite exist, because I, like anyone living in an Anglo-dominated society, had been told repeatedly that the two worlds did not intersect.

I've always had a thing for fantasy and fiction. I'm human—we have a thing for what we call "stories." Yet I don't really involve myself in many of the books, movies, games, and comics that are out there, because I began to notice something unnerving, boring, and upsetting about what took up the most space in fantasy fiction, specifically this aspect of the ever-timely socially outspoken genres of sci-fi and cyberpunk: they're actually kind of joyless.

Growing up, I somehow missed reading many of the dystopian-fi classics my peers are familiar with; a school-to-school shuffle might be part of why. I dodged *Animal Farm* and *Brave New World*. I know *The Time Machine* only as a distant family flick. *A Clockwork Orange* is "that film they made me watch in school," and I didn't bother picking up *1984* until a few years ago. Once I got the gist, I didn't even feel like finishing it. (I skipped to the end. Nothing of value was lost.)

Perhaps this makes me uneducated, but perhaps this is why I am here, able to write this to you, an echo of the scream I've felt since childhood: Storytelling Is Magic.

They say satire is dead, and I would agree. I think the past several years—an entire decade actually (at least)—has been a long, crescendo-ing funerary procession for satire, for the idea that you could point to meaning through a story and that the general reaction would be one of understanding instead of a groping, fumbling focus on the characters and not the moral. It is as if hyperindividualism has caused people to be so egocentric that they can't see past the actors to the meaning. Cautionary tales are, in my opinion, six feet under, buried by the apathetic cognitive dissonance of a society that thinks every character must be some sort of hero or role model, a winner to some loser. A society that fails to understand that not every fantasy is functional, not every daydream is entirely separated from nightmare.

A society that has been made to forget just what fiction and fantasy *are* on a fundamental level. Imagination has atrophied into commodified distraction from the lives and world it was made to benefit. People rewatch, binge, and reminisce over the same escapes on repeat while their own lives lack creative attention.

Warnings in the form of story are taken only as entertainment and often are emulated instead of analyzed. Quick, how many times have you heard of a company using the term "Midas" to describe their fantastic product, completely overlooking that Midas's tale was a tragedy? How many people casually idolized that douchebag from *Wolf of Wall Street* even though the entire movie was a hideous downward spiral focused around a predatory capitalist—the literal liberal boogeyman of our age?

Does anyone really need another grisly fantasy narrative with orcs or fairies trotted out as an escapist musing on racism? Does it actually help us to listen to some white man's detailed retelling of real-world colonial oppression where only his avatar makes it out alive?

Now how many people obsess over zombie apocalypses, sci-fi dystopias, and cybernetic armageddons?

Did any iteration of Mad Max inspire people to become climate activists?

How many people, on average, feel like the world is ending?

And, last question: Compared to escapism and doomsdayism, how many dystopias experimented and resolved with functional solutions to the real-world problems they were based on?

I believe that dystopia as a genre is outdated and obsolete in our day and time, watered down to a literary category and the backdrop to Hollywood blockbusters. With every iteration, this has just mentally conditioned people to see dystopia as inevitable and apathy as the only logical response.

For years I've read countless books and op-eds on society falling apart, but again and again they stop short and offer notions of mitigation or rebuilding, because that's largely missing from our social mythology! "Imagination" as a mental faculty is being wildly misused, if not intentionally downgraded.

Cautionary tales are only useful when they are read as such. Warnings are obsolete when the very thing they warned about has already come to pass. There is no point in bringing up dystopian writings now, in the full midst of climate crisis!

We are in a car teetering on the edge of a cliff. Dystopia as a genre is the sign half a mile back that reads "Dangerous Curves Ahead." And way down at the foot of the mountain are Indigenous people that warned us not to pave a road to the peak.

So now what?

Understand that "imagination" is not some miraculous quality of children's books or simply an attractive fantasy theme. Imagination is conception; it's where consciousness models and prepares for possible outcomes. Imagination is the ability to render in the mind an image of immaterial reality! In our minds, we can create that which does not yet exist: thus do all our works, stories, and inventions arise "from nothing." At its simplest, we can use this ability to guess at outcomes, create new tools, and plan for the future. At its most complex, we use this ability to worry, fantasize, delude ourselves, find meaning, create, and problem-solve. Each of these happen in the imaginative mind, and *we can only do one at a time.*

What are we spending most of our time on?

Book after movie after series after comic book uses fictive space as a place for social daydreaming and oft-fetishistic escapism instead of play-fueled brainstorming. We end up dazzled by the mass fantasies and coerced into forgetting that they—like all story in human society—are meant to express something *meaningful* beyond just the vicarious excitement of someone else's dramas, someone else's sufferings, someone else's victories.

Imagination is a realm of endless possibility that offers one the ability to see past the conditions of the present into the bigger picture of probable outcomes. Many people are rightly focused on the creation and critique of media as an expression—a psychological pressure valve—of a person or society's anxieties and fears. But there is more to fantasy and fiction than being used as a broadcasting vehicle for our shadows and anxieties, just as there is more to us than our fears and traumas. At a time when we as a society are becoming more aware of the *function* of story, this should be remembered as we grope for solutions in an ever-crumbling reality. We all suffer when an arbitrary boundary is placed between play and problem-solving.

Have we forgotten that play is a form of teaching and learning *as well as* relief and expression?

We must ask ourselves: What is being done with the attention we give to media? What are we getting out of it? I feel that there's something lost when story loses its mythic and educational use and is seen solely as a form of entertainment and play, and it cannot be forgotten that the downgrading of fiction from meaningful mythos to commodified entertainment is the extended work of colonial culture.

The idea that fantasy and reality do not intersect is not only racist and sexist in its applications and historical appearances, it is also a skillful tool of disempowerment.

Imagination is "just" play, and fantasy is "just" entertainment ... so is worry "just" worry, with no effects on our reality? Our health? Is planning, also, nothing but a daydream to be discarded? Surely you can tell where I'm going with this. At some point, it becomes apparent that we've often been tricked into ignoring what our minds have to say, dissuaded from being brave enough to engage with our hopes and fantasies as if they were things that mattered. When you apply intent to fantasy, it becomes a seed of radical creativity.

Please, listen to me: everything ever done or created was imagined first. Before we make anything, it is first a dream.

So let's talk about the future.

Here we are, fully enmeshed in a "dystopian hellworld" and wondering how to survive. Escapism rots with tradfash dog whistles while the vast majority of folks struggle to make it through another day in the real-life slow-pocalypse of late-stage capitalism and ecocide. We awaken to the Anthropocene and must find our way to what comes next.

The rise of active, critical solarpunk as a genre of both social discourse and world building is a great example of how daydreaming and fantasy can be used to create real-world solutions for us all. But when the average person sees the imaginative realm as a thing to be exploited for fantasy fulfillment only, its capabilities for offering and becoming so much more than that are squandered in favor of immediate gratification. Even among socially aware writers and role players, for instance, so few people can figure out how to create worlds without recreating all the same problems as this one. Fantasy settings where magic and dragons can exist, but rape, poverty, and racism can't be omitted. You know, because it's "realistic."

If we cannot even be bothered to *imagine* realities in which these problems are solved—or even nonexistent—how could we expect that the Powers That Be will just automatically create such a world for us?

Our reality is limited by that which we decide is unimaginable. I suggest to all that we expand and exercise our imaginative abilities—because our enemies have not hesitated to imagine, plan, and enact what we may consider "unthinkable."

Again. You do not accomplish that which you do not first imagine.

What now? Move forward with your imaginative faculties fully engaged and properly utilized. Recognize imagination as a creative problem-solving space and respect it as such. Remember that there is no distinction between worry, planning, and daydreaming except that one unknowingly attempts to plan for the negative, the second knowingly plans for the future, and the third can create the incredible if only we first believe that it matters. My suggestion to you all is to take stock of the stories you focus on and ask yourself how they are—or are not—serving you.

Not sure where to go, what to imagine, how to work your way to a livable future? I offer to you the concept of "Metatopia." Metatopia derives from both the self-referential creative concept "meta" and the state of maturation and growth suggested in metamorphosis. Metatopia is not defined by an enforced aesthetic, nor is it derivative of social anxieties. Rather, it is defined by being a constructive social fantasy done with the intent of influencing the real world to create societies where equality, liberation, and joy are fundamental aims.

To begin with, you'll need to figure out just exactly what you want. Use what you hate, what we suffer from, and what we oppose in our activism as a compass to the world you desire—shadows can tell you where the sun is. Examine your fantasy for unturned stones and residues of social traumas so often taken for granted for something to be realistic. Are there still hierarchies? Is there still poverty? What happens to someone down on their luck? What pressures and hardships are people facing and why?

Often lurking in the corners of fantasy realms is the fact that many people find suffering and struggle deeply entertaining; basic writing advice warns that a story without any critical drama is boring. It's far more appealing (or just plan "realistic") to many to imagine a world in which heroes fight evil overlords than one in which people have the power to avoid social corruption. People are far more likely to swoon over romanticized toxic codependence than drool over a world where equal access to resources and a lack of gender roles makes white knights and tragic princesses obsolete.

So a tip: *Dare to imagine peace and safety. Know that this will take faith.*

As our world begins to heal from the collective traumas of oppression, society must learn to trust letting go of the addictive familiarity of what hurts most and get comfortable with growth and peace. Apart from religious dogma about the term, I define *faith* as the fidelity of one's attention to an outcome—literally, how long you can sustain giving something your time and energy before doubt makes you quit. Faith is mandatory for applied imagination the way it is for growth, because so often, the act of imagining and actively creating our desired realities requires that we endure and persist without immediate evidence that a difference is being made.

I shall leave you with one last question. You have heard that this is your story, and you have a right to decide how it goes.

Do you believe in yourself, as the writer?

If not, start. Our world depends on it.

Addendum (July 27, 2020)

The question I have asked could not be more urgent. As you know, in the time between writing this piece and its publishing, the outbreak of the COVID-19 pandemic has thrown societal collapse into overdrive and put a burning spotlight on the oppression and mindless cruelty built into the colonio-capitalist way of governance. As many other BIPOC voices are echoing, one of the most crucial roadblocks to social change is the crisis of *imagination* that we currently face.

When routinely and systematically stripped of the full expression of their humanity, forcefully disconnected from land, and deprived of what they need to fully thrive, people become trapped in survival mode, too poor in time, money, energy, and spirit to afford the seeming risk of hope, imagination, or exploring the unknown.

But we are now firmly in the chaos period: the uncomfortable interim of societal collapse, the lightning-struck tower, the great shuffle.

Even familiarity lacks comfort, for our familiar comforts have either been lost to us or proven deceitful. We have no choice, then, but to drive ahead, carry light into the darkness the way our Ancestors have done time and time again, thrust forward by (if nothing else) an inability to safely stay put.

Re-creation

It is on us to imagine, plan, build, and re-create; and let us do so with joy. Write, draw, chat, dance, and sing yourself into a new future. Ask yourself what you *really* want, weave your community close to the earth, and find out what possible futures are ready to be born from love and intent, cocreated by you and those around you. Where fear and doubt lurk, shine on them with the spotlight of your own consciousness and ask: *who does it serve for me to think this way?* Let us come together in a great renaissance of thought and action to build Metatopias on the ashes of our dystopic present.

No matter what happens, you can afford to dream. This is your birthright. Use it

About the Contributors

Anonymous does street art and loves dogs.

Aubrey is a licensed clinical social worker in the Midwest. She's worked in the child welfare field for fifteen years, in a direct service role for seven years. She works with adolescents in foster care, focusing on increasing their connections to birth and chosen family so they can enter adulthood with a community that will unconditionally love and support them through every good, bad, and dramatic decision of young adulthood.

Cecilia Bahls is a former stripper/grumpy Cancer currently stomping around Portland, Oregon. She works in a variety of media, including hand-drawn and digital illustration, intaglio printmaking, and rug making. Contact her at cecilia.o.r.bahls@gmail.com for info about commissions.

Beyondeep, also known as G, is cofounder of Beyondeep Productions and is a Black, queer, and trans multidisciplinary artist. They produce erotic films and art to empower and spread love. Follow their work at @beyondeep and @ArtistGabrielle on social media.

Matilda Bickers is an artist and writer originally from Boston's South End. Her experience in sex work, which she entered at age eighteen, has enabled her to focus on art and activism and the vital intersection of the two. She has performed her written work at the Radar Reading Series in San Francisco and Sister Spit in Portland, Oregon. Witnessing the experiences of other people faced with only terrible options in a world uninterested in their success or even survival, Matilda has worked to create spaces to amplify and showcase their creative work, from *Working It*, a quarterly zine of sex worker art and writing, to the annual Portland Sex Worker Art Show. Matilda is currently writing and illustrating *Aspiration Risk*, a graphic novel about her ongoing attempt to leave the sex trades for a career in health care and the painful parallels between the two industries.

peech breshears writes stuff and currently resides in Kansas. They study and write about comics, graphic novels, American Black history and culture, and erotic labor history.

Leslie Bull is a poet, a mother of five, and a grandmother of ten. Leslie specializes in harm reduction and addictions counseling. Her work/ life is based in lived experiences in drugs, street life, and prostitution. These days you can find Leslie traveling around in her '83 Vanagon with her faithful sidekick, Dajeh the dog.

Ellis Burnheart is a musician and visual artist with a BFA from Pacific Northwest College of Art. She is a former stripper, webcam dominatrix, and phone sex operator who now works in the field of accounting. You can find more of her work at www.EllisBurnheart.com or by following @ellisburnheart on most social media.

Phoenix Calida is a former sex worker turned public speaker and podcast creator and host. Her lived experience in survival and street-based sex work as a queer Afro Latina and survivor of sexual violence and police brutality has molded her into an outspoken advocate for antiracism, income equality, and sex workers' rights. As a WOC with chronic illness and mental health issues, she is a passionate voice for mental health visibility, access to care, and speaking truth to gender and racial bias within health-care frameworks.

Camille has numerous hoe names but currently goes by Muva Dragon on the Internet. She lives in the Carolinas as a queer mother in a marriage between two loving human Aquariuses. She is the daughter of an abolitionist and a drug dealer turned truck driver, the granddaughter of a former field hand and an army veteran, the great-granddaughter of an enslaved mother of thirteen, and great-great-granddaughter of a midwife. She loves her lineage and her proximity to royalty and embodies her ancestral power in all that she does when she can.

Melissa Ditmore, PhD, is an independent researcher and scholar. Her book *Unbroken Chains* (Beacon Press, 2023) focuses on the roots of human trafficking in the United States. She has written numerous papers and reports about the sex industry and edited *Encyclopedia of Prostitution and Sex Work* (Greenwood, 2006). Find her at www.melissaditmore.com.

Eden entered into sex work as a stripper in the very last days of 2005 and retired in 2011 after working in several states. She did some cam work and is currently contemplating a return. Eden is an anti-Zionist Jewish licensed clinical social worker (LCSW) currently serving the veteran population. Enjoys reading, writing, playing the piano, and dancing. Currently working full-time and also organizing with Santa Feans for Justice in Palestine. Proud wife of an IBEW member and proud kitty mama of Mel Bel.

Elizabeth Juarez is a sustainable and ethical fashion designer, stylist, and artist. She is also a sugar baby and has been in this line of work for two and a half years. She identifies as lesbian and looks at sugaring like any other job—she just gets paid a lot more than a "regular job." Her goal as an artist is not only to spread sustainability and ethics, but to enlighten people on the topic of sex work and to give sex work the credibility it deserves. Art and ethics go hand in hand, and it's her pleasure to help spread awareness.

Stephanie Kaylor is a PhD candidate in the Department of Feminist Studies at the University of California, Santa Barbara. They are the founder of the Sex Workers Archival Project and the reviews editor of *Glass: A Journal of Poetry*.

Crystal Kimewon is a member of Wiikwemkoong Unceded Indian Reserve. She holds a bachelor's of Indigenous social work from Laurentian

University, where she also minored in the study of sociology. She is currently pursuing her MSW. Though she's not likely to share this with you in first meeting. Crystal is known by her community for walking in her truth: if it can help another person along their own healing journey, there is nothing she is not willing to share.

Nick Lovett is a Black nonbinary artist from West Oakland, California. You can find more of their work on Instagram at @blackgirlsaregod.

Dee Lucas is, like many, a nonbinary diasporic femme activist, ritualist, multimethod performer, and adult model living in unceded Seminole Territory who is focusing on hustling the way toward Land Back and obsessing over the Universe in their spare time.

Janis Luna (she/they) is a stripper forced into early retirement by COVID-19. She now works as a freelance writer and sex-worker-affirming therapist, and she misses the club (but mostly the dressing room) every day. She can be found at @janis_therapy on Instagram and at www. janistherapy.com.

Manon is a dilettante who likes to overwater plants. A Bay Area native, she has worked as a stripper in Los Angeles since 2013 and as an escort across the country and internationally. She has also been a house painter, a kindergarten teacher, an English tutor, an art school dropout, and a semiprofessional gambler, and she has always loved to write and draw. It is an absolute honor and privilege that her first-ever published writing and drawings are included in this groundbreaking anthology. Everyone who contributed to this revolutionary book shines a unique and illuminating perspective on the nuances of sex work in such an impactful way. Manon is overjoyed to have been a part of this vitally relevant and beautifully curated project. She is forever in awe of all sex workers.

Monty Monster Slayer was a dancer for four years and an artist out of the womb. Monty's art transforms her bitter and humorous energies into a celebration of women's strength and beauty. Unbeknownst to them, the actions of swine-like sex work consumers and critics would become fodder for her pieces, which elevate the female form and experience through representational figurative art.

Naomi, inspired at once by radical philosophers and tulips, is looking for beauty. As a mechanism for change and a source of inspiration, Naomi uses beauty as the driving force behind her activism. With a focus on consciousness raising and creating "insurgents," Naomi uses media of all forms to change how Black women interrogate culture and the systems they interact with on a daily basis. From the big boogeyman of capitalism to increased access for abortion, there is no subject too taboo for conversation. Naomi is concerned with world building in the truest sense. A Texan at heart, she's especially impassioned about spreading this energy through the South: as a means of completing ancestral business, and working in a long line of women committed to making the world suck less for their families and communities. She can be found on Instagram at @newnegrowomanhood.

xaxum omer is a single mother, poet, painter, musician, sex worker, and independent scholar. A long-term Brooklyn resident, originally from Los Angeles, they've been vagrant since giving birth, living where life allows across the continental United States. They are slowly making their way back to the Korean countryside, where they lived with their mother as a very young child, refusing to settle until.

Alyssa Pariah is a Black Puerto Rican trans woman from New Jersey. She became an activist in 2009 at the Audre Lorde Project's first Trans Justice Community School. Since then she's volunteered with dozens of groups, trying to help forge solidarity across groups fighting particular oppressions with the organized left.

Rambling Hooker is a self-taught artist based in the Bay Area. Like many sex workers, they have worked in multiple subcategories of the adult industry for well over a decade. They began drawing short comics as an outlet and hobby in 2017.

Leila Raven is a Caribbean queer mama and community organizer who worked on the campaigns to end the criminalization of sex work in Washington, DC, with DecrimNow DC and in New York with Decrim NY. Her work has focused on organizing queer and trans people of color to develop community-based strategies for building safety without policing. She is the former director of Collective Action for Safe Spaces

(CASS), and in 2020 she was a cocreator of the 8 to Abolition platform, which offered actionable steps that cities can take to move toward the abolition of prisons and policing.

Domino Rey is a stripper, writer, speaker, labor organizer, and medical professional. Their work has been featured in *MEL* magazine, *The Face* magazine, and the *Los Angeles Times*. They have organized workers' rights education and unionization campaigns across a variety of workplaces and industries. Areas of clinical interest include harm reduction and street medicine for people engaging in street economies.

Adrie Rose is a Pittsburgh-based freelance writer, portrait photographer, and photojournalist focusing on sex, health, Black life, and Black culture in the Rust Belt.

Sage is a gender-fluid stripper. They were born and raised in Chicago and graduated from college in Washington, DC, with a BFA in theater technology. While doing jobs in their field of study, they became a sex worker to supplement their income. That has led them into aerial, burlesque, drag, and embellishing exotic dancewear and tour costumes for other performers.

Kat Salas is a proud Chicanx and member of the Apache Nation. Her practice seeks to explore the ways in which curating can be used to build platforms for intersectional conversations and take up space in academic or institutional settings. In her spare time, you can usually find her tattooing around Portland or collaborating on the latest project for the Sex Traders Radical Outreach and Liberation Lobby (STROLL).

Sarah is a former trans sex worker from Australia.

Scarlett is a stripper, mother, and artist from Portland, Oregon. Her art generally focuses on using symbolism and occultism to portray abstract ideas centered around her experiences of being a sex worker. She also draws directly from her own experiences at work. She uses the devil form often to portray the demonization and stigma of working in the sex industry. She can be found on Instagram at @shnazzy_.

Susan Elizabeth Shepard started stripping in 1994 in Austin, Texas, and continues to dance as her body allows it. She is one of the cofounders of *Tits and Sass* and has written for outlets including the *Missoula Independent*, *Willamette Week*, *Texas Monthly*, and *Pitchfork*. Her essay about working in a North Dakota strip club during the Bakken fracking boom, "Wildcatting," was a Best American Essays Notable Pick in 2014, she received an Oregon Literary Fellowship in 2018, and she is the only person to simultaneously hold awards from the Montana Newspaper Association for sports reporting and the Erotic City stripper awards show in Portland, Oregon. She lives in Portland with her spouse and cat. She can be found online at susanshepard.com and at @susanelizabeth on Twitter.

Sky Rocket is an artist and dancer with the memory of a goldfish and the hibernation patterns of a North American black bear.

Molly Smith is a sex worker and activist with the Sex Worker Advocacy and Resistance Movement (SWARM). She is also involved with Scot-Pep, a sex-worker-led charity based in Edinburgh, which is working to decriminalize sex work in Scotland. She has written articles on sex work policy for *Guardian* and *New Republic*.

Cisqo Thyme is not ready for her close-up.

Jelena Vermilion is a trans-femme full-service sex worker, porn performer, archivist, and activist of almost a decade who lives with disabilities. She has limited experience being incarcerated, being homeless, working outdoors and on the street, and as an undocumented migrant. She now works primarily out of her rented residence. She has been featured in several national media outlets advocating for decriminalization. Jelena is the executive director of the Sex Workers' Action Program of Hamilton (SWAP Hamilton) and and successfully set a precedent by bringing a cop to justice by having him charged and demoted after she was assaulted. She provides professional trainings and public speaking engagements for organizations and agencies who wish to affirm the rights and dignity of sex workers. Notably, Jelena has lectured at McMaster University's School of Labour Studies and the University of Guelph's School of Social Work. In 2018, she was subpoenaed as an expert witness in the *R v. Boodhoo* case, a constitutional challenge to certain sex work laws in Canada. As of March 30, 2021, SWAP Hamilton joined twenty-four other member groups from all over Canada, along with the Canadian Alliance for Sex Work Law Reform, and launched another charter challenge to the majority of the current sex work laws (Bill C-36/ PCEPA). Her website is www.Isis-Intrepid.com/about.

Emily Dall'Ora Warfield is the nom de guerre of a sex worker, BDSM educator, advocate and organizer, erstwhile researcher, and sometimes writer based in the New York City metro area. By the time you read this, she will have graduated with her MSW and will hopefully be doing something she doesn't totally hate for money. She's published essays, poetry, and reviews for *Mask, Ache,* and *Tits and Sass,* a blog by and for sex workers. She is also the author (under another name) of the super-fab cult hit mega-zine *Girl with the Most Cake: The Lori Adorable Story* and has relaunched her zine-making endeavors at FairySlipperPress.com.

Eva Wŏ is a queer biracial Chinese/white multidisciplinary artist working with collage, GIF, and social practice. They create lush and lawless dreamscapes that function like freedom spells, combatting outdated notions of respectability and desirability by conjuring fantasies of liberation. Consistently censored for transgressing boundaries and blurring elitist determinations of sexist acceptability, the work is both joyous and obscene. Their practice is visionary science fiction defiantly celebrating queer and trans BIPOC and sex workers as worthy protagonists and depicting inclusive possibilities of what could and should be in a world without shame and violence. As both a response and a demand, their art imagines a vivid utopian future of uncensored sexual and gender self-determination for all. Born and raised in northern New Mexico, they have lived in Philadelphia for a decade. Wŏ was awarded the Leeway Foundation's Transformation Award for artists demonstrating a long-term commitment to art for social change and has been the recipient of the Leslie Lohman Artist Fellowship, the Center for Emerging Visual Artists' Visual Art Fellowship, the Elsewhere Living Museum Exchange Fellowship, and the 40th Street Artist-in-Residence Program.

ABOUT PM PRESS

PM Press is an independent, radical publisher of books and media to educate, entertain, and inspire. Founded in 2007 by a small group of people with decades of publishing, media, and organizing experience, PM Press amplifies the voices of radical authors, artists, and activists. Our aim is to deliver bold political ideas and vital stories to people from all walks of life and arm the dreamers to demand the impossible. We have sold millions of copies of our books, most often one at a time, face to face. We're old enough to know what we're doing and young enough to know what's at stake. Join us to create a better world.

PM Press
PO Box 23912
Oakland, CA 94623
www.pmpress.org

PM Press in Europe
europe@pmpress.org
www.pmpress.org.uk

FRIENDS OF PM PRESS

These are indisputably momentous times—the financial system is melting down globally and the Empire is stumbling. Now more than ever there is a vital need for radical ideas.

In the many years since its founding—and on a mere shoestring—PM Press has risen to the formidable challenge of publishing and distributing knowledge and entertainment for the struggles ahead. With hundreds of releases to date, we have published an impressive and stimulating array of literature, art, music, politics, and culture. Using every available medium, we've succeeded in connecting those hungry for ideas and information to those putting them into practice.

Friends of PM allows you to directly help impact, amplify, and revitalize the discourse and actions of radical writers, filmmakers, and artists. It provides us with a stable foundation from which we can build upon our early successes and provides a much-needed subsidy for the materials that can't necessarily pay their own way. You can help make that happen—and receive every new title automatically delivered to your door once a month—by joining as a Friend of PM Press. And, we'll throw in a free T-shirt when you sign up.

Here are your options:

- **$30 a month** Get all books and pamphlets plus a 50% discount on all webstore purchases

- **$40 a month** Get all PM Press releases (including CDs and DVDs) plus a 50% discount on all webstore purchases

- **$100 a month** Superstar—Everything plus PM merchandise, free downloads, and a 50% discount on all webstore purchases

For those who can't afford $30 or more a month, we have **Sustainer Rates** at $15, $10, and $5. Sustainers get a free PM Press T-shirt and a 50% discount on all purchases from our website.

Your Visa or Mastercard will be billed once a month, until you tell us to stop. Or until our efforts succeed in bringing the revolution around. Or the financial meltdown of Capital makes plastic redundant. Whichever comes first.

Patriarchy of the Wage: Notes on Marx, Gender, and Feminism

Silvia Federici

ISBN: 978-1-62963-799-0
$15.00   152 pages

At a time when socialism is entering a historic crisis and we are witnessing a worldwide expansion of capitalist relations, a feminist rethinking of Marx's work is vitally important. In *Patriarchy of the Wage*, Silvia Federici, best-selling author and the most important Marxist feminist of our time, asks why Marx and the Marxist tradition were so crucial in their denunciation of capitalism's exploitation of human labor and blind to women's work and struggle on the terrain of social reproduction. Why was Marx unable to anticipate the profound transformations in the proletarian family that took place at the turn of the nineteenth century creating a new patriarchal regime?

In this fiery collection of penetrating essays published here for the first time, Federici carefully examines these questions and in the process has provided an expansive redefinition of work, class, and class-gender relations. Seeking to delineate the specific character of capitalist "patriarchalism," this magnificently original approach also highlights Marx's and the Marxist tradition's problematic view of industrial production and the State in the struggle for human liberation. Federici's lucid argument that most reproductive work is irreducible to automation is a powerful reminder of the poverty of the revolutionary imagination that consigns to the world of machines the creation of the material conditions for a communist society.

Patriarchy of the Wage does more than just redefine classical Marxism; it is an explosive call for a new kind of communism. Read this book and realize the power and importance of reproductive labor!

"Silvia Federici's work embodies an energy that urges us to rejuvenate struggles against all types of exploitation and, precisely for that reason, her work produces a common: a common sense of the dissidence that creates a community in struggle."
—Maria Mies, coauthor of *Ecofeminism*

"Federici has become a crucial figure for young Marxists, political theorists, and a new generation of feminists."
—Rachel Kushner, author of *The Flamethrowers*

"Federici's attempt to draw together the work of feminists and activist from different parts of the world and place them in historical context is brave, thought-provoking, and timely. Federici's writing is lucid and her fury palpable."
—Red Pepper